Dancing about Architecture and Other Ekphrastic Maneuvers

DANCING ABOUT ARCHITECTURE
and Other Ekphrastic Maneuvers

edited by Oz Hardwick
& Cassandra Atherton

MADHAT PRESS
CHESHIRE, MASSACHUSETTS

MadHat Press
MadHat Incorporated
PO Box 422, Cheshire, MA 01225

The Library of Congress has assigned
this edition a Control Number of
2024932890

ISBN 978-1-952335-76-1 (paperback)

Edited by Oz Hardwick and Cassandra Atherton
Cover design by Marc Vincenz
Cover image: collage by Bob Heman

www.MadHat-Press.com

First Printing
Printed in the United States of America

Table of Contents

Introduction

We live in an age of information overload and sensory saturation, the edges of our attention constantly clawed at by the next TikTok reel or Tweet. If, as Aristotle claimed, the aim of art is to represent not the outward appearance of things, but their inward significance, how do we access that significance when the gallery, the museum, and the concert hall have all become seas of waving phones, all vying for the perfect shareable shot of the moment's celebrated surface? Although this is a question we didn't ask when inviting contributions to this collection, it's a question that many poets have answered in their responses. Artworks, or representations of artworks, have never been more easily accessible, with even the most obscure work discussed in these pages a mere click away – what would Plato have made of digital repositories and installations? – leading to increasingly complex engagements between viewer (or auditor) and art.

As a famous quotation of untraceable origin has it, "writing about music is like dancing about architecture." It's a clever, provocative observation which, while ostensibly commenting on the futility – impossibility, even – of music criticism or melophrasis, also invites us to think about both the relationships and the marked divisions between distinct artforms. In invoking these inter-art juxtapositions, it effectively conjures them into existence: who can read this without imagining the possibilities of an architectonic jig? This, of course, is just what the arts do: they are forms of magic, calling things into existence which did not previously exist and may not even have been imagined.

The ekphrastic endeavor is particularly striking. Approaching the same observation through a different medium, for example, Dominic Symes, in discussing "gallery" ekphrastic poems, suggests that "the poet's lived experience in the gallery space produces the poem, as an after effect of the poet's failure to provide a comprehensive translation of the artworks contained within a gallery."[1] Ekphrasis, then, may be

---

1. Dominic Symes, 'A "Meandering" Line: The Effect of Indeterminacy in a Gallery Ekphrasis', *Axon* 8.1 (2018). https://www.axonjournal.com.au/issue-14/%E2%80%98meandering%E2%80%99-line

considered as that which occurs at the point at which representation of an artwork breaks down – an accident of impossibility, as it were. It might be experienced, as Cassandra Atherton and Paul Hetherington state, as "a contested and uncertain space where the poet may not hope to fully interpret or re-represent an artwork but may contrive to yoke two (or more) modes of perception into a new poetic formulation."[2] In this way, the ekphrastic encounter is characterized by its liminality and sublimity. David Kennedy's influential work describes this occurrence in terms of "the performance of a complex temporal relationship" between an artwork (or collection thereof), the writer, and the reader, which goes beyond mere description or translation from one medium into another, and remains in a state of constant flux and potential.[3]

Ekphrasis forms a prominent and adaptable thread in contemporary poetry, from individual poems to full collections, and in specialist journals such as *The Ekphrastic Review* (https://www.ekphrastic.net) and one-off projects such as Nathan Langston's collaborative work *Telephone* (https://phonebook.gallery). This vibrancy of the form and its current renaissance is also attested by a number of critical studies. For the present volume, we approached a number of international anglophone poets to write an ekphrastic response to an artwork of their choice, accompanied by a short commentary on their poem. Artists' reflections on their own practice are, we believe, particularly valuable as they provide context and insight into their creative intentions and processes. For this reason, we gave our contributors free rein in deciding how they went about approaching their commentaries and articulating how these poems came into being.

We should note here that, while the term ekphrasis is most commonly used in relation to writing in response to a work of visual art, the eighteenth-century coinage more generally connotes

2. Cassandra Atherton and Paul Hetherington, 'Ekphrastic spaces: the tug, pull, collision and merging of the in-between', *New Writing: The International Journal for the Practice and Theory of Creative Writing* (2022). https://doi.org/10.1080/14790726.2022.2025850
3. David Kennedy, *The Ekphrastic Encounter in Contemporary British Poetry and Elsewhere* (Farnham: Ashgate, 2012), p. 3.

a description of – or commentary upon – any work of art in any medium. So, while James A. W. Heffernan's monograph, *Museum of Words: The Poetics of Ekphrasis from Homer to Ashbery* (1991), is still one of the most famous works on ekphrasis, his definition of ekphrasis as "the verbal representation of visual representation" is now out of step with contemporary practice.[4] Consequently, dance, music, video and indeed the architecture mentioned in the title, are amongst the artistic media with which the works collected here engage in creative conversation.

And what of the inward significance? Where does that lie in the rush and chatter of the 21st century? What these very diverse responses seem to suggest is that, even though the nature of our engagement with art – and even the nature of our engagement with the world – may be transforming at a dizzying rate, art continues to provide us with transformative encounters which both consolidate and illuminate our sense of our individual selves and our shared humanity. And the artworks of the poems themselves, too, provide the occasion of such encounters, inviting us to look anew at the artworks to which they respond and, significantly, to look anew at ourselves.

Are you dancing?

Oz Hardwick and Cassandra Atherton

---

4. James A. W. Heffernan, *Museum of Words: The Poetics of Ekphrasis from Homer to Ashbery* (University of Chicago, 1993).

Luke Kennard

Go Tell it on the Mountain

after Jonah Preaching Before Nineveh, *John Martin, (Oil on board, c. 1840)*

Moses started sentences with 'So', used *like*
excessively, was like, I'm like: *literally*.
It winnowed out the tedious. I mean it.
So you get up there, you stumble on the dais,
you get up there with no idea of what you're going to …
We learn from Spinoza that many of the prophets
had debilitating speech impediments.
Start there. God puts you in a gallery,
God puts you in a private collection,
God dusts you off and reaches for the corkscrew.
But me, I like to ride the vulture, I like
to get out in front of the big Waterstones,
dim colosseum, sky brochure apocalypse,
parody of the big reporter. I was there.
I am infirm, I will have my rescuer,
I will live to play with the minibar
on life's vast promontory. Brothers and sisters,
sometimes when I'm being human
I try to say something to make you feel okay,
an animal whose job it is to cry for everyone,
and every act of cruelty, lack of care, or worse.
A little malice in the canteen, dim traductions.
What's shocking is what drives it in the first place;
I have been to the first place, I do not talk about it.
Talented artists wax indignant on the reproduction.

There are so many photos now – one year would be
a life's work for a full-time archivist, crumbs
in the creases of their corduroy; one day they'll quit,
burned out and nothing done or gleaned,
about as useful as a politician. Side-saddle
on a wooden dog. But like I said, you've caught me
at my worst, I didn't sleep last night,
these are the minutes for your approval does anyone
have anything to add? No? So let's move on.

Commentary

My initial impulse was to write about *The Legend of Zelda* or *Succession* or whatever else I was currently fixated on, but I felt disingenuous. There are too many brilliant contemporary examples of ekphrasis that draw on videogames or pro-wrestling or R&B for me to feel like I had much to add that wouldn't feel like a dim tribute. It's wearing to see this treated as a novelty in the wake of works like Morgan Parker's *There Are More Beautiful Things Than Beyoncé*, Stephen Sexton's *If All the World and Love Were Young*, and Ross Sutherland's *Street Fighter II* sonnets. If there's any argument left to be made around the role of 'popular culture' in poetry it feels unedifying to keep having it. Obviously what sets the good stuff apart is that it goes far beyond an act of fandom and effortlessly transcends the wink-to-the-camera 'bet you weren't expecting a poem about *this*' posturing; but those are the pitfalls, and they're deep. Maybe those are always the pitfalls, whatever the poem we're trying to write, along with the aforementioned fear of creating worthless sophistry, the dim tribute, something which lacks life or the force of its own logic, or that glisten of shame, that critical sense of *something at stake*. Impelled speech, urgency. That's all I ask for; the rest I can tune into.

I've been trying to finish a manuscript about the Book of Jonah for the last four years—loosely as a kind of follow-up to *Cain* (2016), and involving the kind of research and pseudo-scholarship which has become my favorite displacement activity. I have over a hundred pages but it's largely terrible and I recently came to the conclusion that I had, in fact, barely started, or at least was only just beginning to understand what the collection was supposed to be. A low-res print of John Martin's *Jonah Preaching Before Nineveh* has been on my wall for a while. The funny thing about the Book of Jonah is that: 1. the prophecy works, everyone repents and, much to Jonah's chagrin, the city is spared destruction; and 2. We don't get to hear a *single word* of the prophecy itself. The opposite is true in every other prophetic book of the Old Testament: the text is entirely the content of the prophecy, delivered in first person by the prophet themselves, and it doesn't work at all (hence Lamentations).

Martin's paintings are far from the highest rated among his generation, but I love them for their almost decorative, set-design qualities—part Byzantian ikon, part movie backdrop—and for the sense of scale, the way we have to crane our necks to take in the scene—vast edifices, the grand buildings of a dictator. Art historian Max Adams draws out the political dimension of this aesthetic: "Martin liked to open his play right in the middle of the drama, just like a modern movie director: he drops us into the action so that we are part of it, believe we can be part of it. Martin is inciting us to tear down the house; but we are certain, as participants, that we start at the bottom, as Martin had."

I've always loved the strange phrasemaking of poetry, the feeling that you have to dive down into some part of yourself that uses language in a different way—I like how close that can feel to a sort of linguistic divination, fitfully illuminating. I'd not written anything for months before being prompted to write this poem, and ekphrasis felt like the best way to get back into the project, wrestling with the idea of what a prophet even is, or ever was, let alone what the function might be today. It's something sort of funny and sad, the utter conviction of delusion or vice versa, or something that surrounds us but speaks in a language we can't understand.

COLE SWENSEN

Deer Bloom

There's a deer bloom in the oak grove; petal by petal, with each eye more open, they watch us pass with a hint of suspicion, but with a larger one of humor, which we can't quite come to admit is derision.

Deer bloom among oaks, a kind of soft dawn, a refracted fawn, radiating into day. It's the stillness that emanates from their watchful bodies—even when startled, leaping up, alarmed, there's yet something so orchid about them, something waxed in the calm of their aloft. I was walking up a trail last week and was interested to see, so many times, the mark of a deer's hoof emphatically disrupting the imprint of a human shoe, often smearing it beyond recognition.

Though most deer bloom only at night—it's the ambient sounds that are out at that hour that allow them to flower. Innumerable and untraceable, yet they enable them to open, to bloom even among their predators, and, in fact, to bloom right in their faces—coyotes, mountain lions, etc. Disguising yourself as a flower is an extremely effective protective mechanism because the predator is never prepared for the fact that you can, and do, simply get up and walk away.

Commentary

I've been intrigued by the possibility of using ekphrasis as a way, not only of writing on art, but of turning what you're looking at into art, of creating a transformative perspective, an attitude that fundamentally alters what it's looking at. Some things leap out and suggest this approach—branches tossed about by a storm are readily seen as dance, a used bookstore is pretty easily seen as a museum, a cemetery as a sculpture garden, etc. For the final project in one ekphrasis class that I teach, students have to write a series of five poems that display the artistry in something most people wouldn't think of as art. A student one year wrote on an evening at her busy restaurant as an opera (comic and tragic by turns); another wrote on her outrageously messy room as installation art, another on a tornado as land art, etc.

This piece is not as direct as those examples, but in my mind, it's looking at sleight-of-hand as an art and deer as particularly accomplished practitioners. Through the art of magic, they are able to transform themselves into flowers and thus protect themselves from their carnivorous predators.

I wrote it one day as I was walking in the hills north of San Francisco and saw some deer nestled under some oaks, languidly following us with their eyes as we walked by. I grew up around deer and realized that I'd often been struck by their astonishing calm—*their faces as placid as flowers*—or something like that rang in my mind, and I followed that first impression through an (il)logical progression to see where it would lead.

The slip that underpins the poem is based on a kind of faux or specious logic, which I've been working with a lot over the past few years. I'm attracted to it because, on the one hand, it confronts the absolute absurdity of our contemporary world and our refusal to apply even the most basic logic to our enormous political, social, and climate problems, while on the other hand, focusing on absurdity allows us to engage in a kind of humor or optimism, in spite of it all. I'm interested in this approach, not because I think there's anything even slightly humorous in our current situations, nor that there's any possible cause for optimism, but because I think that depression is a dangerously debilitating state, one that makes us increasingly unable to respond to contemporary challenges with the needed energy and conviction, while hope and optimism, however achieved (i.e. through specious means) can be very useful in maintaining a spirit capable of imagining change and facilitating it.

The problem with faux or specious logics is that, while being utterly ridiculous, they still have to work. In the case of this piece, the trick-logic comes to a head at the end: *Disguising yourself as a flower is an extremely effective protective mechanism because the predator is never prepared for the fact that you can, and do, simply get up and walk away.* The predator supposedly sees the deer both as prey and as a flower—and why isn't that illusion broken as "the flower" gets up and walks away? The phrasing has to present the image without raising the question or has to keep the question in suspension until the reader is out of the poem and on to the next thing, so that it never gets asked.

In light of the comments above, clearly I think that more structures that prevent the asking of necessary questions—for instance, in this case, questions that would reveal the false logic in operation—are very much not what we need right now, but perhaps in that light, such structures in poetry can also serve as a metaphor for and a pointer toward exactly that—the fact that many structures currently in place (most of them profit-based) are designed to prevent us from asking necessary questions.

HELEN IVORY

The Original Bad Girl

Lady Lilith, Dante Gabriel Rossetti 1887

We've seen your faces, Lilith
this one sanctioned by the Brotherhood.
It is unimportant you began with one face
yet by the time the paint had dried
you were someone else.

No, not someone else – that's not the point.
You are an *Enchantress;* you don't wear socks
or nip to the shop for a bag of potatoes.
This is your rectangle of pictorial space;
these are your flowers, torpid with symbolism.

That bad girl attitude you sometimes wear
translates here as *narcissism* –
Oh, you love that mirror
and how it takes you in.
Dante can't get a fair shake, poor lamb.

He's done that thing with your hair
so that you're inviting the viewer to feel the tension
as the locks are pulled taut
and one can imagine them springing back
like a fiery trap. Then you're done for.

Commentary

I am writing about witches at the moment for my new collection *Constructing a Witch* (Bloodaxe 2024). I have been wanting to write about Lilith for some time and Dante Gabriel Rossetti's *Lady Lilith* was a good way in. I have called her *The Original Bad Girl* as a play on the idea of 'the original sin', which of course relates to Eve. In Judaic mythology, Lilith was Adam's first wife. She was banished from the Garden of Eden and branded a "she-devil" – a sexually wanton, baby-stealing monster (typical witch behavior) – because she refused to obey him.

I have a visual art/cultural studies background and the Pre-Raphaelite Brotherhood are very familiar to me. They aimed to reintroduce Romanticism and the spiritual back into art and wanted to get back to the values of art before Raphael – who they felt corrupted art with a mechanised approach to painting. 'Brotherhood' of course suggests a male environment – they did later let one or two women into the company but most of the women involved with them were muses, models, wives, or lovers, and appear to be interchangeable commodities acquired by the Brotherhood. They referred to such women as 'stunners' – one of the prerequisites of these 'stunners' was the long flowing hair which is associated with seduction and sexual awakening. Think "Rapunzel, Rapunzel, let down your hair." Rossetti originally attached these lines from Goethe's *Faust* translated by Shelley to the frame of the painting:

> Beware of her fair hair, for she excels
> All women in the magic of her locks,
> And when she twines them round a young man's neck
> she will not ever set him free again

I like the double meaning of 'locks' and wanted to include that in the poem. I also wanted to focus on the shifting faces both of Lilith – who has been depicted countless times – and on the fluidity of these 'stunners' who were not living, breathing women at all but an idea or vision of Woman; The Enchantress. I felt it important to allude to the fact he started off with Alexa Wilding as *Lilith*, and in the repainting substituted her with Fanny Cornforth.

I wanted to write the poem in a tone that I know that Rossetti would hate. It crashes right through his Medieval and idealized ideas of spirituality and beauty and confronts him. It takes him to task on his loaded symbolism with the flowers and such (the white roses symbolic of cold love, the poppy of forgetfulness – poor lamb!). I couldn't quite get anything in about the about those strange erect candles in the mirror and their odd reflections, but I will note them here. It would have been too much in this poem – it may appear elsewhere as an image. In the writing of this poem, and others I have written for my witch book, I have tried to temper the anger that compels me to research and write, into something which I hope has a little more wit.

SARAH HOLLAND-BATT

Saturday Evening: Fairfield Porter

Here it is always 1964—
the lawn composing itself

in lemon and celery,
lilypads and slabs of light

that form and reform
around the elms surging

in their darkness, hurricane
windows thudding on cladding

and the boy who turns toward
the grey and white house, turns toward

and away, looking in at the rooms
of his life, that strychnine stillness

of glass vivisecting space
into neat rectangles,

nothing unseen, nothing uncontained,
the roses incarcerated in their jar,

adjudicated by transparencies,
the water's warped ring

sure as the whorl of a fingertip,
dragging the world

into rankled demon shape,
even the curling ivy wallpaper

bent by time, towards and away,
and that white house floating

on a cliff's edge, threatening to fall,
and the boy outside, looking in

at the neat coil of an armadillo rug
like a corpse in an empty room.

Commentary

This poem began, as many of my ekphrastic poems do, with inner searching: the question of why I have found myself drawn to a particular artist or body of work. This is not always immediately evident to me at the outset of writing; I find an ekphrasis, more often than not, is the opportunity to think through and test the cause of my fascination, to probe my own aesthetics and taste.

In writing this poem, I was interested in considering the aesthetics and techniques of Fairfield Porter's work, and what it has to say about a certain kind of American wealth and comfort. I initially became interested in Porter due to his proximity to the New York School of poets, including James Schuyler, Frank O'Hara and John Ashbery, and the thematic and stylistic echoes I saw between his work and those of another artist from the same milieu who also intrigues me, Jane Freilicher. I had first encountered Freilicher's work at an exhibition in New York a decade ago, which paired her work with the poetry of the peers in her circle.

Porter, like Freilicher, is a painter whose work is already inextricably in conversation with poetry; he was also the son of a poet. Curiously, in spite of his proximity and friendship with Ashbery, Porter insisted on representational painting, during a time when abstract expressionism was at its zenith. I find this countercurrent of his work intriguing, not least because, in addition to being representational, it is also relentlessly quotidian, and has a nostalgic patina. It is a body of work that seems to exist outside its own time; seen from today's vantage point, it seems to memorialize a vanishing, utopian form of childhood and adulthood in spacious homes and green spaces that is increasingly only accessible to the privileged classes.

Porter mostly takes as his subjects either interiors (rooms, domestic scenes) or the genteel yards and houses of Maine, populated with figures who are at ease in their environments. There are echoes of Hopper in some of the canvases, insofar as they seem to surveil figures who are unaware they are being observed. The scenes he conveys project a sense of safety, security, and cosseted comfort. There's a sense that the human figures are preserved, not only in paint, but by their wealth. Porter himself came from money; he owned an island in Maine, Great Spruce Head, where he hosted artists and writers, as well as other properties. The largesse and easefulness in his canvasses belies an ease he enjoyed in his life, I suspect. And yet his paintings have their own charm. They are careful and observational, paying intense attention to shadows and light, and also draw heavily on a recurrent dark forest green that at times communicates a sense of darkness and peril.

My poem is not a strict one-to-one ekphrasis of an individual work, but rather an amalgam, drawing images both real and invented from a range of his canvases. Most closely, it responds to a 1972 painting, *Under the Elms*, which shows the figure of young boy standing in the dappled light of a garden, downslope from a house, but it draws on aspects of other paintings too. In my poem, I hoped first to capture some of the quality of Porter's eye: the fracturing of light and shadow on grass, as well as the slightly suffocating domesticity that suffuses his work, and the sense of something dark lurking beyond all that light. I wanted the poem to probe at the question of what, exactly, Porter's work memorializes and feels nostalgic *about*: a vanishing world, one in which childhood goes on forever and death does not exist—which is, in its own way, a more terrible fate.

Pascale Petit

Concert for Motherhood
after Rebecca Horn

If I say my mother was a piano I mean the grand
    in the children's home where I clung to one leg.

I'm old enough now to raise the lid and look at the strings
    and hammers inside, the harp of her nerves

as I try to recall tunes she played to me
    when I was in her body. If I say my mother was a piano

I mean the way the keys would turn into shark's teeth
    with one twist, and the grand would be hanging

from the ceiling upside-down, opening and closing
    its jaws trying to tell me something that must never

be set to music, something my cells remembered
    when they were brain-coral, my hands dead man's fingers.

Commentary

Rebecca Horn's kinetic sculpture *Concert for Anarchy* is a powerful metaphor and I have long wanted to write a poem in response, but was unable to for many years. I'd look at my postcard of it and feel baffled how to interpret such a weighty but disturbing image – it seems so complete and like a poem in itself. The upside-down grand piano which hung from the ceiling disgorging its keys always brought back my shock at walking under it as it cranked into action and exposed its discordant torrent of fangs, the lids opening as if to announce chaos.

One day I looked hard at the postcard, and at videos of Horn's piece in action. Frida Kahlo's enigmatic painting title, *What the Water Gave Me*, popped into my mind – I've written a whole collection of poems based on her paintings and called it *What the Water Gave Me*. What did the piano give me? I'm not musical, but when I was nine, I asked my grandmother for a second-hand one. She wrote to my mother and relayed my wish, but it did not materialize, we simply couldn't afford it, so I can't play the piano or read music. Beyond the field at the back of Gran's council house was a farmhouse, where there were roomy bedrooms with beds we could bounce on, and an upright piano. I'd hammer away at the keys, making much the same noise as Horn's sculpture!

Then it came to me. I saw a flash of myself aged four, sitting on a cold tiled floor, when I was in a children's home in the south of France, clasping the leg of a grand piano, hoping for my mother to visit.

I started writing the poem, fascinated by the insides of the beast – that harp and hammers. I still didn't quite understand how they worked, but I quickly did some research. What if the piano was my mother? I tried to write about my most terrifying feeling – being inside her, in her womb. I had always been frightened of her. She was severely mentally ill, but I didn't realize this until I was eighteen. Looking back at my poem now, I guess that *Concert for Anarchy* is as unpredictable as my mother was when she was on a psychotic high, disgorging her secrets to a roomful of partying families and their children.

The piano's cascading keys must have conjured my poem's open-mouthed shark, perhaps it's the seven-headed apocalyptic 'beast from the sea'! I end up drowned and sea-changed, an antediluvian embryo. It's impossible to be in a gallery under Rebecca Horn's strangely animate piano and not watch it go through its anarchic riot, flouting the cultural setting and upending our civilization.

IAN DUHIG

Text at an Exhibition

I

Celtic letters were named for trees;
from such windthrown timber pulp
I launch an ink-caulked paper boat.
All at sea, looking on its reflection,

it's clear I've got this back to front:
its wake, like fanned clinker planks,
peels back to its keel, one line alone,
quatrains to monostich, then is gone.

My draft reverts to unvoiced breath,
a ghostly watermark on blank sheets
disappearing like a shape in the sand
from wreckage the foam blows over.

The sculptor's craft can tack to this.
What seems her flotsam at a glance:
ribs circling a spine of air, oak sails,
resolves so we see each mobile turn

into a world and its circumnavigator,
a vessel boxing the compass of itself,
its own cargo, ports, voyage and you,
the sculptor and I: we're all its crew.

II

See her living sculpture turn back on
itself like a sonnet or this poem, now
chasing its own möbius strip of a tale,
swerved to become the word 'mobile'

at 'i' – yew in Celtic, a light pun only
working off the page and heard in air,
as a mobile leaves its plane to become
gravity-defying art sprung from wood.

You can blow smoke end-grain to end-
grain through a flatsawn red oak plank
like meanings through a poem. Smoke
with mirrors make magic too: a mirror

held at a sick mouth to mist was a test
of death but also opened doors beyond
like misty lake surfaces once for Celts.
Two facing mirrors reflect on infinity –

worked by your facing breath, this art
and poetry reflect on your reflections,
lives in your eyes, dies when you turn
as all breath turns to mere air at death.

Commentary

Breath Water Marks

> *To most people who look at a mobile, it's no more than a series of flat objects that move. To a few, though, it may be poetry.*
> – Alexander Calder

> *Nothing is more beautiful than water.*
> – Andreij Tarkovsky

I'd enjoyed working with sculptor Juliet Gutch on the successful *Dovetailing* multimedia installation at The Manor House in Ilkley in 2021 so I didn't hesitate in accepting when she invited me to become involved with her new project, *Breath Water Marks*. She explained that it came about because, after Ilkley, *Dovetailing* moved on to the Windermere Jetty Museum; Juliet spent time in the adjoining boatyard and conservation workshop, where they are renovating the recovered hulk of *Ferry Mary Anne*, once used by Wordsworth. Alert to her environment, she particularly noticed the patterns of wakes left on the lake water. She began photographing them, manipulating those images and ultimately making mobile sculptures inspired by these figurations.

I think Juliet imagined I would be drawn to *Breath Water Marks* because of the Wordsworth connection (the work will eventually be shown at the Wordsworth Grasmere Museum) and of course I was. But I was also attracted by the challenge of writing about sculpture inspired by water, exploring in-between states, provisional worlds created by the mobiles but never fully occupied by them as their motion continually redefined their topographies. Even when *Breath Water Marks* is ready for exhibition, it will still exist in a condition of permanent becoming – inevitably and correctly, given the task's central paradox: taking water and making its beauty fly.

The notion of a ferry between worlds also transported my imagination; I could visualize Wordsworth's ghost still aboard, keen to explore more 'unknown valleys' from it as he had done when a boy. Windermere is in an ancient Celtic part of England, Cumbria, and for Celts, lakes were portals leading to the Otherworld. That belief features in my poems because Juliet's mobiles embodied for me the idea that movement is life, as it was for Aristotle; the wood of her sculptures still like trees, animated by wind. I often watched them slowly turn and return, worlds winding and rewinding histories like Yeats's gyres. Yeats' phrase from 'Byzantium' turned through my mind as well: 'I call it death-in-life and life-in-death', its echoes gathered meanings as *Breath Water Marks* developed.

As I mention in my poem, Celtic letters are named from trees and this was a way of infiltrating the essence of the mobiles with the essence of poetry. Walcott spoke in an interview once of 'the essential cube that really is the poem' and my boxy quatrains reflect something Juliet wrote for *Dovetailing*: 'Each mobile hangs from a point of the cube within which it explores all the different potential configurations'. If these comments sound as if from the world of mathematics, the element inspiring them is of a very different nature, water. This is the same paradox as in poetry, the pull of language's music against words' stubborn insistence on meaning, that tidal flux and reflux which is both blessing and curse to the poet.

Poets on these islands have historically been inspired by water, a tradition going back at least to the Old English poem 'The Seafarer' in the tenth-century *Exeter Book*. Images connecting water and language are so well-established as to be clichéd: the babbling brook, someone gushing their enthusiasm and so on. Taking the ferry back to Ireland, I'd stare at the passing sea for hours: the water seemed to me like fire in its shapeshifting power, but also wind and music played freely – a reel, perhaps. Music is frequently associated with water in many forms; the title Juliet chose for her project alludes to breath marks, symbols in musical notation indicating a slight pause, putting me in mind of the glottal stop employed by sean-nós vocalists that might represent the singer being overcome by the emotion of the words, a moment of plangent tranquility in the middle of an overflow of powerful feelings.

Those held breaths, my own before Juliet's moving, beautiful sculptures, I now see as tidal pulses of life foreshadowing its end. That all art is created against death is hardly an original thought, but one whose truth seems plainer as I age. The end of my poem here alludes to Fulke Greville's *Caelica 83:*

> You that seek what life is in death,
> Now find it air that once was breath.

For this poet and Juliet's mobiles there are intimations of immortality in nature's cycles—she often uses recycled wood. But we live in a time seemingly intent on fouling nature's engines: the UK's rivers and seas are being poisoned by sewage. At heart, *Breath Water Marks* is a celebration, not only of water's inspirational beauty, but of water clean enough that you can see through to new worlds, worlds that have always been there, will always be there if we can draw back from destroying them permanently.

Jane Yeh

Self-Portrait as Claude Cahun in Jersey

Deep blue eyelids painted on, an enormity of ruffles.
Depending on the light, I'm theatrical or pert like a chihuahua.

My story is typical: girl gone bad, *un chien malheureux*.
I washed up here like a starfish or a drowning slut, legs

And arms akimbo. Better the devil than anonymity
In some attic, painting flowers. Like a bouncy Pomeranian,

My ambition couldn't be restrained by a harness. Better
The devil they know than an uneaten slice of strudel.

I can stay underground like a canny potato until it's time
For me to emerge. My story is a murder mystery in reverse:

I was a detective, then a corpse. I came back to life
As a hypothetical person – one part startled milkmaid,

Two parts candelabra. To be snug in a bungalow
Was never an option. My hair is different from my hair

The way a body differs from a body. In a mirror, *you*
And *me* are the same word. Better the double you know

Behind the camera. Better a camera than a naked eye.

Commentary

This poem is a kind of sequel to another ekphrastic poem I previously wrote, 'Self-Portrait as a Double Exposure', which the editors of the magazine *Dilettante Army* had commissioned as a response to the photograph *Que me veux-tu* (1928), by Claude Cahun. I'm embarrassed to admit I hadn't heard of Cahun prior to that, but on looking up more of her work I became intrigued by another photo of hers (untitled), which led to the writing of this poem, 'Self-Portrait as Claude Cahun in Jersey'. I was drawn to this second photograph by its costumey theatricality, how the clothes and makeup seemed (based on what I'd read about Cahun's lifelong rejection of gender binaries or norms) like an ironic, slightly comical parody of femininity.

In writing an ekphrastic poem, I usually depart from the image or initial inspiration pretty quickly, partly because I always worry about boring the reader of a poem—it seems perhaps too pedestrian or obvious to simply focus on the artwork, or the true story of its making. I hope this doesn't sound egotistical, but I'm more interested in making up my own story around it, or (often) a story quite tangential to it. One metaphor for how I'd describe this is what quantum physicists call *entanglement*, where two particles somehow remain connected, even when separated by vast distances. (Thanks, Caltech Science Exchange website!) I would say my poem is entangled with Cahun's photograph even though it also exists completely independently (you don't need to know the photograph or anything about Cahun). To borrow another scientific term, I could call Cahun's work a catalyst, which in chemistry means a substance that causes or accelerates a chemical reaction while itself remaining unchanged. (Thanks, various online dictionaries.) That's probably a more accurate analogy for how an artwork (which in my practice includes TV programs, music, etc.) can spur me into writing a poem.

I wrote the opening line of this poem based on my memory of the Cahun photograph, without looking at it as I worked, so it's really about my perception of the photo, the impression it made on me; an interpretation of it rather than a description. The rest of the poem doesn't refer to the photograph at all (apart from the phrase 'startled milkmaid'). In my early drafts I tried to write each line as a complete sentence, so that every couplet would consist of a pair of self-contained sentences— the concept of the form was to embody the way the photograph consists of two figures, both of whom are Cahun (through her use of in-camera double exposure; a number of her works employ the same trick). Unfortunately, after a while, the form felt forced and repetitive, so I had to sacrifice it to the needs of the developing poem. The idea of doubling stuck with me, however: in the past, I've hardly ever used anaphora as a device, but admiring other poets' skill with it made me eager to try it more. In this poem I thought the pairs of sentences starting with 'Better …' could be considered a subliminal nod to the doubled image of Cahun in her photos. So, in a sense the poem has ended up being entangled with the photograph that inspired it, but not in the way I intended.

ANDY JACKSON

The Cripples
L. S. Lowry, 1949

He wanted to paint a window, but couldn't stop
    it becoming a mirror (on him, or you). You,

    who may also have *a very queer mind*
drawn to the shapes bodies make
        with factories, poverty and war

        over their shoulders, who may also
be *attracted to sadness* and feel like them (us).
    Not that it's another world. I mean, I

    keep seeing myself there on the left,
in the smoky middle-ground,
        though it's not like me to place my hands

    on another man like that. Am I pleading? Or
    claiming him as ballast? Haven't I noticed
the hook poking out from his sleeve?

Admittedly, there's a lot to take in, composed
    as it is of ordinary human pathologies –
    children pushing each other, curious, the rest of them
    (in one way

or another) hunched over in the cold air, getting on.

The figures in the distance are blurred into
                    the particulate grey. Are they moving

                    towards us or away? Some days,
looking into the frame, I can detect, like
            the thinnest of cobwebs, all the sticky, projected

            threads of our denial. Now, which cripple are you?
                    Or which will you be?

note: the two italicised phrases in the poem are quotes from LS Lowry

Commentary

The window that is also a mirror

The opening sentence of 'The Cripples' could apply to any painting. To any sculpture, film, performance. To any poem, for that matter. You could say that everything I write – everything any of us write – is partly about what it's looking at, and partly about the particular way of looking that it relies on.

~

Ever since I first saw L. S. Lowry's work, I admired it, was drawn to it. It's hard to say precisely why, but it was something to do with his subjects, thin figures, their bodies like saplings, vulnerable, but in postures that suggested movement, a kind of Anglo getting-on-with-it that reminded me of my mother. It was also something to do with his palette – dust, smog, cloud, brick, pigeon feather. Lowry's work felt, to my body, democratic.

So, it shouldn't have come as a surprise to encounter his 1949 work *The Cripples*. Is there any more democratic assemblage of people than the disabled? It's not, of course, at all representative or genuinely diverse. Visual art tends, as we do in our ocular-centric culture, to emphasize that which can be seen. Deformities, prosthetics, scars, atypical ways of moving around.

But the painting came as a jolt because disabled people are rarely foregrounded. If we are, it's often as individual calamity or heroism, not as a collective. In the image, the implication seems to be that we are disabled by the times as much as anything else. Lowry's particular way of looking also seemed to me to include a kind of empathy, albeit mingled with disavowal. It's

28

illuminating to read him quoted as saying, 'I feel more strongly about these people than I ever did about the industrial scene. They are real people, sad people. I'm attracted to sadness and there are some very sad things. I feel like them.'[1]

~

Pronouns and names are critical ways of seeing, too. *I feel like them* is a way of drawing close and pulling away. I am not immune from this, too (I have replaced the *they* of an earlier version of this essay with *we*). Nor are you. This is why we are both present in my response to Lowry's painting.

The word *Cripples* is part of the jolt of the work, his and mine. It's a word that goes back to at least the tenth century and has been woven tightly together – double-helix-like – with ableism, the implication that bodily difference can disqualify a person from full humanity, rather than being an illumination of an essentially human precarity and diversity. But words can change, be broken and remade.

Lowry once also said, 'Accidents interest me – I have a very queer mind you know. What fascinates me is the people they attract. The patterns those people form, and the atmosphere of tension when something has happened ... Where there's a quarrel there's always a crowd ... It's a great draw. A quarrel or a body.'[2]

I'm interested in more than quarrels and bodies. Or, I should say, I'm interested in looking at what can't quite be seen, or what only emerges through acute sensitivity, humility and patience. What lurks behind quarrels, within bodies, underneath words.

---

1. Quoted in Ramachandran M, Aronson JK. 'The diagnosis of art: Lowry's cripples.' *J R Soc Med.* 2007 Mar; 100 (3):153-4. doi: 10.1177/014107680710000315. PMID: 22135840; PMCID: PMC1809168.
2. Ibid.

JANE MONSON

Circles

for Howardena Pindell

The earth to the wheel. The yellow underground line or an empty plate on a table. The moon full cycle or spots behind the eyelids when you've looked at the sun too long. Feeling stuck. The painted hole in a cartoon, that lifts like a rug or can't be passed through. A coffee stain, anywhere in the world. Red wine as it runs the stem and marks the base of a glass. Close. Perhaps a stone that the sea and the rocks have defined. A spinning disk of ice above a whirlpool. A tunnel's swallow and release. Fairy circles; footprints of the gods. Lands dotted with poison. The ant death spiral. The way birds often fly; to hunt, stay safe and conserve energy. Rain-pocked snow. Karma. Somebody saying *no;* an impatient *O* before the *K.* Or something else entirely. For her, the circle – she'd learned early on – was something to be feared. Red ones in particular. She saw one painted at the bottom of a glass when she and her father stopped on the road to get root beer in chilled glasses, Northern Kentucky, 1950s. When she asked him what they were, she was told the red circles were indicators, marking the utensils and vessels reserved for Black customers. As an adult and artist she reclaimed this shock, riddle and shape – sometimes unknowingly – in the chads from paper holes, punched out of her mathematician father's hand-held machine, then her own. Thousands of them carefully assembled, laid on the canvas by hand, one by one layering the paper circles until they moved towards and away from you. Some she showed pure, others polluted. Here the red returned – fatal gun shots

– where others were numbered: enslaved, drowned, lynched, tagged. In the next room along, carefully curated circles sprayed under dazzling acrylic – thinned down enough to shower from a can and spread across un-stretched canvas, easy and light as snowfall. Creams and whites sparkle in showers of glitter – one circle holds the next, while settling in relief as they glisten under the moonlight; become a river bright enough to see you safely through the night until morning. This is how she heals. This is how she wants us to heal, after the canvas with the numbers and the cast black hands, cut from the wrists of all ages, some rising up from the gallery's floor, others piled in a hideous state of rest amid the shifting and static sounds of visiting feet: some pausing or returning, others passing quickly, the rest not there or in a process of arriving.

Commentary

This prose poem is an indirect conversation between two artists, exploring some of our processes and methods as shared ground, at the same time as proactively listening to our completely dissimilar experiences and traumas. The commentary is where I want to attempt to articulate the extreme doubts and convictions I experienced while writing both poem and commentary; why and how they played out alongside the relative ease of focusing creatively on the circle in Pindell's work, and in the critical anxiety informing and undermining the writing process and the writer.

For context, last year I went to Howardena Pindell's exhibition, *A New Language*, featured in Kettle's Yard Gallery, Cambridge, 2022, and was left moved, awe-struck, angry and disturbed (not for the first time, but here distinctly), between rooms and beside the pieces themselves, whether canvas, film, sculpture, or video. Why did I write, then publish this poem after the exhibition, while navigating what I will never experience as a white woman? What I can answer here is that I was inspired to write it/it wrote itself while I was moving through the exhibition and in the following months. Prose poetry is how I process and make sense of what can land more clumsily in discussion. That what we don't have in terms of shared life experience, we can still connect through the ways and methods—both critical and creative—we use to process and translate dissimilar kinds of trauma, abuse and injustice. What resonated with me throughout the exhibition was Pindell's story and reflective use of the circle—the experience of her childhood confrontation with this equally benign and complex shape, pure and polluted as she has acknowledged in many interviews, and how that memory—among so many others—informed and focused her life, career, activism, art, and research. In her words: 'We stopped at a root beer stand and on the bottom of the chilled mugs were giant, red painted circles, maybe three inches wide, which meant that they were designated for people of color. As I started drawing circles and ovals, I think I was also trying to heal that earlier experience in Kentucky as a child'.[1]

The journey (muddled and clear), between inspiration, anguish and doubt that I experienced as a viewer and writer is reflected or rather informed by Pindell's expert and brilliantly attentive curating. For her, '… the abstract works are more like an intense relief, a kind of visual healing, so that you get some distance … have a more peaceful or critical way to acknowledge what you've seen. And it helps you maybe overcome some of those deadly emotions that come from being shocked. So, I want people to see … for me making them has a healing side to it.'[2] Pindell's use of art, activism and curating is about healing; this process is as raw as it is defined, and all of that brutal and processed truth needs to be present. For my small part, it's expected that the flow of words within the reassuring, contained square of the prose poem form I'm so familiar with, was checked with constant questions and doubts as to whether I had the right, or should be writing about experiences I'll only ever know are wrong, unjust, senseless and horrifying from the outside. How do I play a role in the conversations Pindell has started and continued verbally and visually?

---

1. Artist interview, Howardena Pindell with Louisa Buck, July 2022, https://www.theartnewspaper.com/2022/07/01/howardena-pindell-interview-kettles-yard-cambridge
2. *Your Self-Care and Wellbeing Support Guide*. Produced by True and Woke for the Fruitmarket and Kettle's Yard, Howardena Pindell, 2020.

When I shared the piece with a few trusted writers, artists, and readers, they focused on the understanding and belief that art is a dialogue capturing, opening and continuing conversations and actions. That it is the work and will of the artist and viewer that the art itself goes beyond barriers and limitations or, in turn, reveals them and then finds ways to transcend and actively move them forward. Pindell asks of herself and the viewer to move from pain to healing as we move through the exhibition, with the awareness that pain and healing will look and be experienced differently by everyone; that her work will elicit a range of thoughts and responses, which is entirely fitting. While I can't know and experience what she has been through, I am familiar with Pindell's process of exploring and translating trauma through an equal amount of attention paid to research and creativity. I can relate to addressing fear and injustice in separate spaces, mentally and physically; one studio for what she calls her issue-related work and the other for her abstract, playful and textural work. Their interplay comes together with all the more impact for being processed in clearly defined contexts. I admire her work and methodology and what that can teach us about the seen and unseen gaps between different lived experiences and the potential bridges we can form across them. I hope whoever reads this, can take from it whatever part of that engagement and manifestation is helpful and that ekphrasis continues to evolve as a framework for these necessary conversations, debates and actions.

Kristin Sanders

She Is a Siren and She Is Sad

The woman in this photograph is always waking up in bed with the wrong man's arms around her. He is very nice, there is no problem, except that he is mistaken, he thinks she is someone else. Her hair like a lion's mane. Her lover beneath the sheets, shy, hiding from the third person in the room, the photographer, just out of the frame. The lover, he has disappeared. And she surges forth, seen twice: reflected above the mantle and in the mirrored armoire door. Split in two like that. One part of her drapes her nude body across the lover, offers him a lie. The other part, her face with its closed expression, eyes downturned, caught in the camera's lens. Which version are you drawn toward? Which version is you? Do you want her to rise from the bed if she's that sad about it? Do you really have anything better you think you could offer her—a world, a touch, a way to feel more full, a lover who is spread atop the bed naked, like a proud animal having made its conquest? But they are friends, the three of them, they could expose all of themselves if they wanted to. It is only the nude woman, who is me, who has accidentally shown what she always tries to hide.

Commentary

"She is a Siren and She is Sad" is based on the photograph *Act Two* by the British photographer Laura Stevens, from her 2023 gallery exhibit *Tu oublieras aussi* ("You will also forget"). Laura is a friend of mine, and I am in two of the photographs in this show. I write prose poetry based on personal experiences, so for this poem I wanted to meld my poetry, which is born from the confessional lineage, with ekphrastic art. And Stevens' photograph allowed me to do just that: to put words to what her photographer's eye understood, which was also something I myself intuited—that there was no desire, no happiness, in this new love affair between me and the man in the photo— but could not yet say. Once, my male poetry professor told me, "Your poetry is smarter than you are." It hurt me then, but now I think it was a compliment and, in fact, the truth. But the best art, no matter the genre, helps us tap into knowledge we didn't know we possessed. The photograph this poem is based on is also smarter than I am. So, my approach was simply to listen to what the image had to say, how the body and face are framed, how the two versions of myself whisper to the viewer. I tried the poem in first person, third person, and second, keeping in mind my desire to implicate the reader as viewer (and as someone who has had their own share of secrets) and to shift the voice at the end—which echoes what Stevens' photo does, revealing the truth as your eyes take in the scene and a story unfolds. I am nude in Stevens' photograph but it is not my body that is exposed: this is a photograph of me that shares all my deepest secrets with the world. That articulates a kind of distance, the distance harbored deep within, which goes untold except for what is shared in the words or images of art. And only a woman's lens, only Laura Stevens, who is in the photo, too, just beyond the frame—only she could have understood, and seen, this truth of what a woman too often gives away, and how we lie, and how deeply we desire something more.

Michael Leong

On Recalling *Diamond Mountains: Travel and Nostalgia in Korean Art,* The Metropolitan Museum of Art, New York City, 2018

for Paolo Javier

dedicated
to the dissent of diamond,
    the Southern School of Chinese painting
found a realm of radiant data ,
        a map beyond
transliterating
            the possible :
            opposite
the steadfast romanization
    of the world,
the work of astronomy-divination
    always records
 colossal lines of republished desire ,
a network of flowers
    extending to the sea :
    as rivers are
technicians of time,
    paintings are not
topographically specific :
    they are
vicarious theories

on how to angle the eye :
there is no
shortage of windows
in Jeong Seon's
narratives of autumn :
birds
preferred their own shadows :
the ocean
sorted   supplementary landscapes
according to lunar postcards
in saffron
and gold :
it takes a small army of bodhisattvas
to translate the ancient analects ,
to impart visual splendor to the
facsimile of dream
:   life is a humble imprint
of a royal library
that archives   a clear and mysterious ode
to floating :
between memory and media
travels the eccentric energy
of duration
: late hatchet : contemporary chisel :
every rock a universe :
every song
a pilgrimage to farewell

Commentary

My poem is a "detail" in the sense that it is "a minute or subordinate part of a building, sculpture, or painting, as distinct from the larger portions or the general conception" (*OED*). It is the final piece—a belated epilogue—to a longer ekphrastic work called "Transmitting the Vertical Immensity of Coniferous Light" that I started in 2018 and had presumed was complete until I reopened the project in 2023. This is to say that the larger poem is a collaboration with myself over time.

"Transmitting" began as a commission. In early 2018, I was approached by Paolo Javier, who was the Program Director for Poets House in New York City. He was partnering with the Metropolitan Museum of Art to organize a poetry event in response to the exhibition *Diamond Mountains: Travel and Nostalgia in Korean Art*. Though I didn't know much about Korean landscape painting, I agreed to compose and then perform a set of ekphrastic poems at the museum. The Diamond Mountains, also known as Mount Geumgang, are located in present-day North Korea and are largely inaccessible to contemporary visitors, which gives representations of them a charged significance. According to the Met, the exhibition featured "artwork from the 18th century to the present inspired by what may be the most famous and emotionally resonant site on the Korean peninsula."

I was working at the time in the English Department at SUNY Albany. Given the expectations of that position, I should have been focusing on my "tenure book," a monograph of literary criticism; but I refused to subordinate my creative practice in favor of more "legitimate" scholarship. I took a three-hour bus ride from Albany to Manhattan—a kind of "renegade" research trip—and toured the show. On a sensory level, it was overwhelming (as museum visits tend to be). I then studied the exhibition catalog, Soyoung Lee's *Diamond Mountains: Travel and Nostalgia in Korean Art,* familiarizing myself with eighteenth-century Korean landscape painting, particularly the perspectival innovations of Jeong Seon (1676–1759). Breaking from the tradition of the Chinese Southern School of painting, Jeong pioneered a style of "true-view" landscape. I wanted to convey something of the density and complexity of his brushstrokes in my ekphrastic translation.

My research suggested a procedure: a six-part poem that mimicked the structure of the catalog from the opening "Foreword" by the Met's President Daniel Weiss to the introduction to the four art historical essays by Soyoung Lee, Lee Soomi, Chin-Sung Chang, and Ahn Daehoe. A sprawling multipart poem—a discursive panorama, as it were—made sense given the fact that, as the show's curator Soyoung Lee explains, "Mount Geumgang covers a vast region. [...] It's not like Mt. Fuji, with that one famous snow-capped peak that gets repeated again and again as an iconic image. Its range is much more dispersed. When Koreans talk about Mount Geumgang, they speak of it as a mountain of twelve thousand peaks!" Mirroring the visual arts, I thought of my extended and segmented poem as a six-panel screen. As a formal constraint, I only used words from the exhibition catalog to form my poem, in homage to both the artists under discussion and the art historians and curators that made such discussion possible. The result was a collaged text that straddled various borders: between poetry and art history, between reading and writing, between surrealist freedom and procedural constraint, between my writerly expertise and my willingness to experiment with foreign materials from a discipline outside my own.

I was pleased, overall, with the end product—and with reading the poem at the Met on March 23, 2018. Indeed, I doubt I will ever read poetry in an environment as beautiful as the Met's Gallery 233 again. A portion of "Transmitting" enjoyed an afterlife after Evie Shockley selected a section of it for the Academy of American Poets' Poem-a-Day series in August 2018. I thought that "Transmitting" might be worthy for inclusion in my next poetry book—but I didn't know where to place it in the manuscript. When the invitation came from Oz Hardwick and Cassandra Atherton to contribute to this book, I realized my uncertainty stemmed from an ambivalence about the poem's ending. I needed another section to close the project.

I wrote "On Recalling *Diamond Mountains: Travel and Nostalgia in Korean Art*, The Metropolitan Museum of Art, New York City, 2018" by drawing on words and marks of punctuation only found in the exhibition catalog's unassuming end matter—the "Notes," "Selected Bibliography," and "Acknowledgments." The piece really started to come together when I chose to utilize some of the many colons from the notes and bibliography; this seemed apt as the colon is a figure of continuity, and the poem a delayed continuation that was five years in the making.

Mary Jo Bang

The Announcement

afer the Cestello Annunciation, *Botticelli, ca. 1489*

A bird came to see me once, a talking magpie
that said, "This will happen"—
and I didn't so much agree as think,

why me? It was arbitrary, as far as I could see.
Ordinary—being at hand and being asked
to do whatever needs doing. Steadfast

as a tattoo that can't be washed off.
A castle that isn't mine reminds me that this
was not my idea, especially considering

how inevitable death is, the way it falls
like a cascading drape from the waist
to the floor, a soft door that works hard—

to keep the world out, and the mind behind it
quiet. I stayed with the clock ticking away,
calling attention to itself and to half-finished

bridges and lilies, and floor-length dresses
that mess with one-point perspective,
and confessionals where men tell men

their stories. Someone had to be used
to exalt the idea of women who submit: a girl
who would agree to say it was an angel.

Commentary

In January 2022, the St. Louis Art Museum—having closed due to a surge of Covid cases—began sending a daily email with a photograph of an artwork in their permanent collection, accompanied by a brief statement about the work. Perhaps because I was working on a translation of Dante's *Paradiso*, where the Virgin Mary plays a significant role, I became curious about the iconography in a painting of the Virgin in one of those emails: *The Madonna and Child with Sts. Louis of Toulouse and Thomas with donors Ludovico Folchi and his wife Tommasa, Davide Ghirlandaio, 1486*. I ended up researching the painting online and eventually wrote a poem in which a speaker makes note of certain elements in the painting but does it as if time has collapsed and she is both in the past and in the present. Soon, another email with a painting of the Virgin arrived and I wrote another poem. At some point, I began to actively search for Mary paintings and to read about Mary's role in Catholic theology. According to the Gospel of Pseudo-Matthew, part of the New Testament apocrypha, when Mary was three years old, she was given to the temple as a "temple virgin" and lived there until she aged out and was assigned to Joseph, who was to act as her guardian and spouse.

I've used the images and my research, as well as my own experience of being a "Mary"—by name and by virtue of some shared experiences—to create "slant" ("tell the truth but tell it slant"—Emily Dickinson) portraits in the spirit of Cindy Sherman's film stills where a costumed figure played by the artist assumes the roles society assigns to women and, in doing so, refreshes our sense of how narrow those roles are.

In "The Announcement," provoked into being by looking at Botticelli's *Cestello Annunciation* (ca. 1489), I painted out the winged archangel Gabriel and inserted a magpie. Magpies can imitate human speech, plus we often say "a little birdie told me so" to describe having learned something that's still unknown to others. The magpie has also been included in other Mary paintings as a harbinger of the sorrow to come (e.g., *Nativity* by Piero della Fransceca).

Botticelli's *Cestello Annunciation* is unusual in that this painting visually encodes a readable vexed interiority, unlike the imperturbable Marys seen in most other Annunciation paintings. Mary's head tilts toward the angel while her body is stopped mid-motion, either turning back toward the book she was reading, or turning away from it. Her hands might be reaching out to touch the angel, maybe to confirm that it's not just a figment of her adolescent imagination—history says she was between twelve and thirteen—or they may be pushing it and its outrageous announcement away. The angel's open mouth emphasizes that it is in the midst of telling, which means Mary is hearing. The angled folds of her red dress and blue mantle underscore the toward-and-away contortion. Unlike in Luke 1:38, where Mary immediately accepts that she, a virgin, is going to bear a child ("let it be done to me"), the ambivalence here is clear and makes Mary recognizably human, which, in the story, she is.

In the painting, a window looks out onto two distant castles and a bridge that goes partway across a river between them. Art critics describe this as the symbolic river of life with the world on one side and heaven on the other. A single tree, its branches pointing up, is read as the tree of knowledge and the wood of the cross. Read that way, this scene is simply the B story in the epic film that begins with the fall and ends with the resurrection restoring Heaven to humans—after it had been lost when Adam fell via an act of disobedience for which, as we know, Eve gets blamed.

I took a moment in a story written between 80–110 CE by an author known as Luke and incorporated Botticelli's more psychologically nuanced reading of that moment—using the elements inside the room and out the window to address what is happening centerstage where a woman is being told she has no power over her body and what will happen to it. The author of the original story appears to have censored out the reasonable suspicion that it was not God who impregnated the young girl, the way the Greek god Zeus surreptitiously impregnated Leda and Danaë, but it was instead a human go-between, priest, bishop or pope, who both planted the seed and delivered the news.

AMINA ALYAL

Afternoon of a Faun

One of the nymphs almost forgets, almost flows herself into grace, but she cannot be permitted, and clicks back to the paper dolls, kinked arms linked, processing, enthralled, in parallel geometries. *Une sonore, vaine et monotone ligne*, they slide past each other, each one a carriage, tracked

empty stage

silence

the flat screen on my desk is, is not Arcadia of a million noons ago, not that Théâtre du Châtelet in Paris, the narrowed stage, it is a film of the show of the show over a century old   it is a silver ping of a triangle like a clock chiming   at the end

rigour   not rigor mortis no   the rigidity of life   not life *aimai-je un rêve?* An oboe underlines the flutes, harps shake out dresses that wish they were papyrus-flat, drinking   a clamouring bank of strings   I want   I want   *désir   je veux   je veux perpétuer* All those intent musicians   still at it now   *aimai-je un rêve?* over a century old   the fleshed nymphs   frieze-dried and this is
this is the secret terror of the flesh

la frayeur secrète de la chair

The nymph cannot be permitted.   Closes her face, lifts her arms, steps till she fits those interlocking devices that slide

48

along a groove   *l'essaim éternel du désir*

he says   when I have sucked brightness out of all the grapes

I will freeze   *je vais voir l'ombre que tu devins*

et que sa volupte d'elle retombe delicieusement en mon âme.
he is still as a bas-relief   taut and erect

tight golden fleece wig   stuck   struck   staccato quick jerk
moving tableaux
watching her sinking realignment as she lays down the scarf he
will take when the blank board vibrates with her gone tissued
self, when worked cloth
lasts longer than blood
every muscle on this stage is stiff   slow   slow   stiff   stiff   slow

seeing them he steps down backwards off the daubed rock,
stealthily stealing
not the poet who sang   not *goat-herd god* nor poet

that swivel of two dimensions
that bassoon   you buffoon   you scarf-scoffing   you scoffing
cock-robin
that very awkward pas de deux   *je veux   je veux   et notre sang*

49

Commentary

Nijinsky's new production for the Ballets Russes, *L'Aprés-Midi d'un Faune,* for which he was a new kind of creator (the master-choreographer), shocked or delighted audiences and critics in Paris in 1912, both for its break with the mime and grace of established ballet and for its overt sexual content. Rodin stood up and applauded, earning himself the animosity of the Parisian press (Järvinen 31). In Nureyev's reconstruction of the original for the London Coliseum (1983), we can see again the way the art draws attention to itself, with its angular, mechanical movement, impressionistic backdrop, narrowing of the stage space, the frieze-like lines of nymphs, and the onanism of the somewhat abrupt ending. The pace and movement follow Claude Debussy's 'continual sliding from key to key' (Zielonka 20) and 'episodes of silence' (19); in this way the ballet realises desire, and the simultaneous cognizance and loss inherent in that state. Some of these intimations are in Keats, that 'incompatibility of time and space' (Krieger 28):

> She cannot fade, though thou hast not thy bliss,
> For ever wilt thou love, and she be fair!

The Faun desires, fails to grasp, rejects art, but creates art, in a tissue of ambiguities and contradictions generated by the mechanical movement and languorous sensuality that clash and yet fuse together in the ballet as a whole. 'Ces nymphes, je les veux perpetuer,' says Mallarmé's opening line ('I would perpetuate these nymphs' in MacIntyre's translation). That 'je veux' remains the theme of both poem and ballet—'I would'—

and in both poem and ballet fulfilment is endlessly deferred, just as Debussy defers it in his prelude.

The ballet is a 'total work of art', combining painting, music, poetry and dance, from French, Russian, Greek and even German sources, claiming as its span of genesis over 2,000 years. 'The idea of a synthesis of the arts was a major preoccupation of the Symbolists', says Anthony Zielonka, 'and the influence of Richard Wagner's idea of the *Gesamtkunstwerk* was central to this interest'. The set and costumes of Leon Bakst (1912) drew on Greek vases, bas-reliefs and Egyptian friezes in the Louvre, and the ballet score was Claude Debussy's prelude (1894), itself a response to Stefane Mallarmé's poem (1865), which the poet had originally conceived of as a play. There is thus an ekphrastic quality, a synaesthetic focus on correspondences, within the ballet itself.

Mallarmé's views on poetry subtly evoke further correspondences, between fleshly experience, memory and art, which in turn are present in Nijinsky's ballet:

> Il n'y a que la Beauté—et elle n'a qu'une expression parfaite, la Poésie. Tout le reste est mensonge—excepté pour ceux qui vivent du corps, l'amour, et cet amour de l'esprit, l'amitié ... Pour moi, la Poésie me tient lieu de l'amour, par qu'elle est éprise d'elle-même, et que sa volupté d'elle retombe délicieusement en mon âme (letter from Mallarmé, quoted Walker 111).

> There is only Beauty—and it has only one perfect expression, Poetry. Everything else is a lie—except for what lives by the body, love, and love in the spirit, friendship ... For me, Poetry takes the place of love, because it is in love with itself, and its voluptuousness falls deliciously into my soul.

So, for Mallarmé poetry expresses beauty, and both are intimately connected with love, bodily and spiritual; and the apprehension of beauty and love, that 'voluptuousness' that 'falls deliciously' into the 'soul', seeming to define not just the tone of the poem but of the music, and of the ballet that ultimately came about from a fusion of both.

My poem, then, is about viewing, on Youtube, a film of the 1983 remake of the 1912 innovative Modernist production, and musing on all the elements that went into that ballet, especially the poem, its own dialogue with classical eclogues, and its constituents of narrative, lyric, and drama (Walker 108). There is therefore a preoccupation with time in my projected viewer, an intuition of the contradictory and teasing elements of mortality and immortality implicit in such a viewing. These elements blend and merge with the ways in which desire is negotiated in the ballet and its rich synthesis of multiple components, something in the manner of Browning ekphrastically listening to Galuppi's Toccata:

> Dear dead women, with such hair too—what's become of all the gold
> Used to hang and brush their bosoms? I feel chilly and grown old.

Works Cited or Consulted:

Text

Browning, Robert. 'A Toccata of Galuppi's' (1855). https://www.poetryfoundation.org/poems/43777/a-toccata-of-galuppis

Code, David J. 'Hearing Debussy reading Mallarmé: Music après Wagner in the Prélude à l'après-midi d'un faune,' *Journal of the American Musicological Society* 54.3 (2001): 493-554.

Keats, John. 'Ode on a Grecian Urn' (1819). https://www.poetryfoundation.org/poems/44477/ode-on-a-grecian-urn

Krieger, M. & Krieger, J. *Ekphrasis: The Illusion of the Natural Sign.* Johns Hopkins University Press, 2019.

Järvinen, Hanna. 'Dancing without Space—On Nijinsky's *L' Après-Midi d'un Faune* (1912).' *Dance Research: The Journal of the Society for Dance Research* 27.1 (2009): 28–64.

V&A, 'Léon Bakst: Design for the Ballet.' https://www.vam. ac.uk/articles/l%C3%A9on-bakst-design-for-the-ballet

Mallarmé, Stéphane. *Selected Poems*. Translated by C. F. MacIntyre. University of California Press, 1957.

Royce, Anya Peterson. *Anthropology of the Performing Arts: Artistry, Virtuosity, and Interpretation in Cross-Cultural Perspective*. United States: AltaMira Press, 2004.

Siegel, Marcia B. "Graveside Festivities," *New York Magazine* 12.16 (16 April 1979): 82-83.

Walker, S. F. "Mallarmé's Symbolist Eclogue: The 'Faune' as Pastoral," *PMLA: Publications of the Modern Language Association of America* 93.1 (1978), 106–117.

Zielonka, Anthony. 'L'Après-Midi d'un Faune: Towards the Total Work of Art', *L'Esprit Créateur* 40.3 (2000): 14–24.

Video

R.M. Productions, *Homage to Nijinsky*, 1978. https://www. youtube.com/watch?v=MgZg80oF2wI.

Jean Saintout, producer. *Nijinsky 1912*. *L'Après-Midi d'un Faune, Poeme Choreographique*, Music Claude Debussy, Choreography Vaslav Nijinsky, Scenery and Costumes Leon Bakst, The Faun Vaslav Nijinsky. Fragments, reconstructed from photographs. 2011. Photography Adolf de Meyer, Animation Christian Comte. https://www.youtube.com/ watch?v=Vxs8MrPZUIg

L'Après-Midi d'un Faune, Poeme Choreographique, Music Claude Debussy, Choreography Vaslav Nijinsky, Scenery and Costumes Leon Bakst, The Faun Rudolf Nureyev. Nureyev Festival, London Coliseum, 1983. https://www.youtube.com/ watch?v=2GqGVkfUip8

SALLY ASHTON

Enumerating the Sublime
after *Thirty-Six Views of the Moon*, by Ala Ebtekar

thirty-six discrete frames arranged on a wall
a circle—white—afloat in cyan blue emerges
the full Moon full of its astonishments
its face broken by rectangle views, by empty space
the human gaze refracted
Earth's familiar satellite
Moon mirroring illusions
we see the there that's not

O

Drink wine and look at the moon
and think of all the civilizations the moon has seen
passing by,
the poet wrote a thousand years ago
how many more have passed by since then
now people build cities on the Moon
we will drink wine and look up
we will see civilizations passing over our heads
how many glasses of wine
how many more will pass
the Moon in pieces looking back

Commentary

I began a serious study of poetry in early mid-life but have been a dabbler in visual arts since crayons, eventually declaring an art major for one semester during my original, what I call age-appropriate, somewhat erratic, college career as an eighteen-year-old, swinging between majors before dropping out in my junior year for 20 more. My artistic dabbling proved just as eclectic. I practiced life-drawing, watercolor, ceramics, jewelry making, woodworking, stained glass, and fiber arts, finding myself years later as a maker of images with words.

Maybe this created a somatic connection to visual art, as professionally untrained as I am, a way of seeing and experiencing a particular work, or at least explains somewhat my pleasure in writing ekphrastic poems.

I also appreciate an assignment. Now, I had one.

Off to the museum I went. I chose the local San Jose Museum of Art because of the title of a current exhibit, *A Point Stretched: Views on Time*, featuring the works of a variety of artists. I explore facets of time in my recent book, *The Behaviour of Clocks*, so I was immediately intrigued. You could say words got to me first.

I'm also obsessed with the Moon. In the first gallery, Ala Ebtekar's collage of the Moon dominates an entire wall; a collage, it turned out, composed of 36 individually framed photographic images of the lunar surface, some overlaid by poems, that collectively recreate an image of the full Moon. Okay: image, words, poets, collage, time, fragments, Moon. That pretty much spells S-a-l-l-y. The shades of blue produced by the cyanotype process used in developing the original also drew me. And eventually the word "cyanotype" itself (blue words?!) stirred something.

When visiting a gallery, I begin by reading the museum's exhibition notes, not only for context to the works on display, but to collect unexpected vocabulary. I might or might not use any such gems in a poem, but I think the practice serves as a pre-writing exercise, sort of like a start button or fuel to seeing.

Though Ebtekar's looming Moon quickly caught my eye, I wanted to make sure not to miss a less physically dominating work and circled the gallery with pencil and open journal, stopping before each piece. That, too, seems like pre-writing, giving myself time to settle and see. To connect. I write in an unlined mixed media spiral sketchbook which also invites doodling or additions of words without fighting directive lines. It gives me a canvas. In a museum, it's always pencil.

I probably spent close to an hour writing margin-to-margin, not shaping lines but capturing impressions. Stopping. Observing. Writing again. Changing positions.

At home, I was surprised at the formal aspects in a first, more traditional lyric draft coming off the museum notes, what I had first imagined might be a prose poem. I know I was playing with word doubling and rhymes, but I also seemed to have composed in fairly regular iambic hexameter rhythm! Weird. With a rhymed couplet at the end, it was like an extended, confused Shakespearean sonnet, dense with observation. Too heavy for the Moon, probably impenetrable to a reader. I needed to lighten it up.

Editing was rather gruesome. Given the first draft, the work became more of a "disassemblage," or erasure, perhaps similar to Ebtekar's approach of piecing the Moon into individual frames. What began as a sort-of sonnet moved to couplets, which additional space suggested a free-line which moved to a freer-than-ever-line. Removing end punctuation and margin justifications further unmoored the poem from its embedded constraints, phrases floating across the page, more and more mirroring Ebtekar's collage. Of course, he was working from an elegant whole, but my original, not so much! My final piece is formatted unlike anything I typically write, but definitely, though somewhat accidentally, in the mode of the original art.

While I did struggle revising the poem, finding its gravity, I see the "battle for mastery" as one between myself and words, to make the felt adequately seen, a translation from visual image distilled through personal perception, transmogrified from experience into embodied words that might equally engage a reader's imagination. My intention is that while the finished poem might complement *Thirty-six Views of the Moon*, which can be viewed on Ala Ebtekar's website, "Enumerating the Sublime" will here offer impact of its own.

Paul Hetherington

Velázquez's Furniture

1.

We approach the Prado, which you size up with an artist's eye. You've come to see the Velázquez paintings, especially *Las Meninas* nodding knowingly to the contemporary world. You talk of King Philip's court: their close, flea-bitten lives and abject colonies. Also, the fire of 1734, burning the Alcazar for days, destroying art – *Venus and Adonis; the Expulsion of the Moriscos.* Russian bombs are falling in Ukraine; Maria Prymachenko's works are threatened – 'I'm possessed by rage'. Walking on the Paseo del Prado, the lurch and taint of history sours the air; the sun might be a crucible of blood. 'Such a glorious conception,' a passer-by remarks, as if to implicate us there.

2.

Las Meninas asks what we observe, as the heaviness of the museum weighs – geometries of space and architecture; idiosyncrasies of light and air; cycling crowds, a painter's perplexing gaze. Your observations shine, as if your words are silvered, yet bewilderment intrudes. Pigments might be artefacts of changing light, imbuing thought, as images gesture at obscure lives – the functionaries in King Philip's court are so much like us boxed inside these rooms. Nearby, Ovid's tale of Minerva and Arachne bustles, all preparation and dramatic irony. The painting's mirror teases what we see; paint washes us backward into history.

3.

We're sucked toward it, like a vortex – a stomach-turning sense of changed proportions. The mirror in the painting widens. We duck under the frame's edge before it knocks our heads; we fall from vertiginous cliffs of seeing – flying clumsily, despite not having wings. We face outwards and the artist's work-in-progress can't be seen. A window shifts, suggesting the time of day, looking to the town. The painting's cup, tenderly placed in royal hands, comes from Guadalajara where the Infantado Palace stands, built through colonial 'trade'. The girl thinks of frothing chocolate.

4.

It draws us into a strange invisibility; a sense of standing within our searching eyes; motes within a widening view. We lie on the canvas's unseen face, being painted by Velázquez, becoming models for his strange ideas. The painting's pottery is warm upon your palm. You sip proffered clove-infused, sweet wine. The scented clay is food for dreams of metamorphosis, even as hunger walks these rooms; even as contemporary words refuse your mouth. Images become a seeing-caress, distributed through many dabbed perceptions. Time quizzes the pigments of our skin, failing to secure them. Your body on a bed mimics Venus.

Commentary

This four-part ekphrastic prose poem, 'Velázquez's Furniture', takes Diego Velázquez's (1599–1660) famous painting, *Las Meninas* (*The Ladies-in-Waiting*) (1656) in the Museo Del Prado, Madrid, as its starting point. This ambiguous and unresolvable work challenges the viewers' sense of what they see, and even of 'reality', largely through its subtle use of perspective. Indeed, it is as if the painting situates its viewers simultaneously in multiple locations; and, furthermore, invites an almost endlessly regressive or recursive contemplation.

Amy M. Schmitter states that '[t]he effect is to construct a viewing position that is somewhat mobile: we might even say that it shifts across the vanishing area from here to there on the canvas's surface' (1996: 260). John R. Searle asks:

> What then is the picture of? Not just of a scene but of how the scene looked or could have looked to the royal couple. But what scene? Well, the scene that includes Velazquez painting a picture of the scene. And what scene is he painting? Well, the scene that includes Velazquez ... (1980, 488)

Central to this understanding of *Las Meninas* is the inclusion in the painting of a mirror, which Albert Cook suggests is 'the key to a veritable system of perspectival repertoires and paradoxes' (1986: 97). The painting opens such a wide variety of questions about how we view painted images and what those images represent, that it is as much a painting about the puzzlements of visual imagery as it is a picture about its putative subjects.

Critics more or less agree upon all of this, although debate continues about what Velázquez had in mind when making the painting, and there also remains disagreement about various aspects of the work, including the nature of its perspectival challenges. For example, Joel Snyder and Ted Cohen assert that 'At the level of its geometry, *Las Meninas* is not paradoxical' but 'thoroughly and ingeniously orthodox' (1980, 430). Notwithstanding such debates, the painting is fertile ground for a poet to consider what representation may reveal— whether in paint or in words—and how the same image may be viewed in various ways.

The poem 'Velázquez's Furniture' addresses such issues by taking up Velázquez's implicit invitation to the viewer to travel in various ways toward, across, around and into the painting. The poem not only transports the reader, sometimes unsteadily, on this journey; it also alludes to the Spanish colonization of the Americas—in this case, of Guadalajara in what is now Mexico. The proceeds from their American colonies funded the Spanish crown, while involving the exploitation, enslavement, displacement and death of countless Indigenous people. It is symbolized in the painting by a cup. Byron Ellsworth Hamann writes:

> *Las meninas* can be linked to the world beyond Madrid, placed within the economic context of mid seventeenth-century Spain and its colonial empire ... More recently, studies of ceramic production in the colonial New World have asserted that the shining red ceramic offered to Infanta Margarita in *Las meninas* was produced in Guadalajara, New Spain (2010, 7)

Overall, my poem is an example of what I would call open ekphrasis; a form of ekphrasis that poses questions about a work of art without trying to resolve those questions, and which also implicates notional viewers in the ekphrastic act. In the second part of the poem, the observation about 'Ovid's tale of Minerva and Arachne' alludes to Velázquez's painting *Las Hilanderas* (*The Spinners*) (c. 1657), also in the Prado, and the end of the poem refers to Velázquez's *The Toilet of Venus* (or *The Rokeby Venus*) (1647–1651). This final allusion reminds the reader that paintings are multiple, just like meanings— and that, as we see one image that depicts a mirror, so we may be reminded of other mirrors in other paintings. Despite the figurative language it employs, ekphrastic poetry may never directly mirror art, but it is certainly able to reflect in complex ways some of art's abiding puzzles and preoccupations.

Works Cited:

Cook, Albert, "The Wilderness of Mirrors," *The Kenyon Review* 8:3 (Summer 1986), 90-111.

Hamann, Byron Ellsworth, "The Mirrors of Las Meninas: Cochineal, Silver, and Clay," *The Art Bulletin* 92:1/2 (March–June 2010), 6-35.

Searle, John R., '*Las Meninas* and the Paradoxes of Pictorial Representation', *Critical Inquiry* 6:3 (Spring 1980), 477-88.

Schmitter, Amy M., "Picturing Power: Representation and Las Meninas," *The Journal of Aesthetics and Art Criticism* 54:3 (Summer 1996), 255–68.

Snyder, Joel and Ted Cohen, 'Reflexions on *Las Meninas*: Paradox Lost, *Critical Inquiry* 7:2 (Winter, 1980), 429-47.

Cassandra Atherton

Forgetting Hiroshima Diptych

1.

after Corpses floating on the river *by Kenichi Nakano*

Nothing happened in Hiroshima. Our story ends before we board the Shinkhansen. You should take back the omelettes, wet with eggy juice, and the miso soup served with three silver pieces of mackerel. We weren't there. We never sat cross-legged prising oysters from their shells; you didn't cry at the museum in front of the keloid suspended in glass. Nothing happened in Hiroshima. Forget me straddling you in the blue of the Seto Inland Sea, your fingers mapping the irregular coastline down my backbone as a new language haunts our lips // Everything happened in Hiroshima. In the deep silence, a mother calls her child's name as they pull bodies with a fire hook from the river.

2.

after the Sakurao still

Late night, you view the city through the pink of a Sakurao gin bottle. You're nameless in the lamp's sepia light, a ghost word in the distillery. I've seen the copper still like a shining missile, its funnel tapering into a golden plume. I've imagined leaving handprints on its surface, playing the oversized flute to hear the fizz of rising bubbles. I can't remember if I drank it straight or on ice, perhaps tonic. Did I take you back to my hotel room, or was it the night I remember slipping down my spine? // Now, as lilac infuses early morning, I try to recall your laddered ribcage, the origin of five small bruises on my thigh. Tangled up in bed sheets, all that lingers is the taste of peppery juniper.

Commentary

My prose poem lies at the ekphrastic intersection between the concept of the nuclear sublime, Marguerite Duras' screenplay for *Hiroshima Mon Amour*, and the Sakurao distillery in Hiroshima. It engages with expressions of intimacy – specifically women's experiences of precarity, impermanence and the unspeakable.

This prose poem begins by investigating Peter B. Hales's definition of the atomic sublime through responding to the drawing, *Corpses floating on the river* by Kenichi Nakano at the Hiroshima Peace Memorial Museum. Hales argues, "The poetics of the atomic sublime might reassuringly couch its explosive potential in the language of nature, still it was a product of man, of culture" (1991: 28). This concept of responsibility is artfully shrouded by connections between the atomic bomb and beauty, awe and the organic, which were originally forged in the media. Hales discusses the mushroom cloud as the 'central icon' or metonym for the atomic bomb, which 'became a man-made marvel of nature ... press[ing] the atom bomb away from man's responsibility' (9). The first part of my prose poem opens with a series of reversals, to challenge this question of responsibility. What happened is slowly erased until the final confronting image of the hook brings the reader face to face with some of the realities of the bombing of Hiroshima.

Moreover, my prose poem foregrounds forgetting, absence and erasure. It uses fractured intimacy to explore women's experiences of sex and love in patriarchy. It writes back to the French New Wave film *Hiroshima Mon Amour* (1959), directed by Alain Resnais and written by Duras. In this film, Carol Mavor identifies the way in which, 'The impossible representation of the dropping of the atomic bomb is understood through sacrilegious love'. She asks the provocative question, 'Can one understand impossible suffering and loss through the erotics of love'? (2012: 14). This prose poem politicises women's survival at the cost of their silence and (self-) enforced forgetting. If Proust famously remembers the past through the taste of his madeleine, in my prose poem the protagonist forgets with the taste of juniper – one of the most pungent flavours in gin.

Finally, as ekphrastic poetry is most often written about paintings – specifically, canonical paintings – I wanted to stretch the definition of visual art in ekphrastic poetry. For this reason, the second part of the prose poem is written about the still in the Sakurao distillery in Hiroshima. It is a huge, almost steampunk, sculpture. Gin is an historically feminized spirit, evident in epithets that have been applied to it: Mother's Milk; Madame Genever; and Mother's Ruin – and in this prose poem, gin is a metonym for forgetting.

Writing about the atomic bomb is always challenging. What inspires me to keep exploring the Hiroshima bombing is Rob Wilson's definition of the nuclear sublime as 'one of the unimaginable, trans-material grounds of a global condition that, paradoxically, can and must be re-imagined, represented, and invoked to prevent this trauma of negativity from happening in post-Cold War history' (1989: 1).

Works Cited:

Duras, Marguerite. 1961. *Hiroshima Mon Amour*; Text by Marguerite Duras, for the film by Alain Resnais, translated by Richard Seaver, New York: Grove Press.

Hales, Peter B. 1991. "The Atomic Sublime." *American Studies* 32 (1): 5-31.

Mavor, Carol. 2012. *Black and Blue The Bruising Passion of Camera Lucida, La Jetée, Sans soleil and Hiroshima Mon Amour,* Durham and London: Duke University Press.

Wilson, Rob. 1991. *American Sublime: The Genealogy of a Poetic Genre.* Madison: University of Wisconsin Press.

JENNIFER HARRISON

Rite of Spring

after Yang Liping's ballet, Melbourne International Arts
Festival 2019

*you should realise that every conditioned dharma is like a dreamy
illusion and an empty bubble, a dew and lightning*
—Vajracchedika-sutra

1. *méi*

Deities descend to the mortal world
attracted by our inner afflictions
and gault confusions
as if love might help us

transcend the empty beleaguered streets
where we lately walk alone or in pairs
to the corner the grocery the bank the bottle-o or nearby park
as if we'd never ventured anywhere before

2. *óng*

They want to help us
reach equanimity's natural harmony
and in her hands a goddess takes the sky's rainbow
like a glorious ensnaring ribbon –

her white white robe
drifts like snow on Kosciuszko –
a small crystal raindrop
falling from her right eye

3. *ma*

Now another merciful incarnation:
the tear hardening to jade-green
proving how hard it is to escape envy
those nights you lie beside me

your arm resting loosely
across mine – and I suppose
that the pity they feel for us is strange
because our eroticisms don't parallel theirs

4. *ni*

Time and space feel like a complex faith
of contradictions
today miming everything and nothing
– persistence and oblivion –

Bodhisattva's small moments
of hand gesture pass into sleep
where we roam in circles – neat and godless –
determined to breathe without destination

5. óng

Beyond the table couch chair bed
pot-plant saucepan balcony
are the small joys of sitting standing leaning
baking loving –

we grow towards the sun
like photosynthesising lotuses
our bedsheets' petals closing – our choreography
of dreams a familiar quilt

6. hóng

My deepening detachment
is not gifted by faith yet slowly grows
roots beneath the wet earth –
onstage a figure dressed in tobacco robes

sweeps up the bodies of the dead
carries wood on his horseshoe back
as he steps over moguls of clay
loughs of dirt – earthly obsessions

7. *méi*

This ballet is a waterhole
an angular black bird with claws raised
against evening's grazing light –
the skittish lizard scuttling through secret deserts –

Stravinsky's music: a vein opening
into jitterfoot leafquiet – moonlight
over campfire smoke – stillness and handpoise –
at dawn we turn to watch a musk duck take flight

8. *béi*

The deities retreat now as if their work
is finished – the edge between soul and body
forever the sound of brittle leaves underfoot
a glass mountain   shattering –

in the morning we rise
as if from trance to find the lotus forest
on the lake being towed away
by the moon's least finite light

Commentary

Le Sacre du Printemps (*The Rite of Spring*), choreographed by Vaslav Nijinsky and composed by Igor Stravinsky, caused a riot when the ballet was first performed at the Théâtre des Champs-Élysées in Paris on 29 May, 1913. Never before had a ballet inspired such controversy. Stravinsky's composition introduced dissonance into popular (or unpopular) classical music and the audience heckled the production, with many walking out in protest. What a delight. For nearly thirty years I've attended every season of the Australian Ballet's productions, initially with an old school friend and her mother, an old friend of my mother's, and never has a whiff of such controversy erupted. My loss, I think.

Rites of Spring: The Great War and the Birth of the Modern Age by Professor Modris Eksteins remains one of the most important books I read as a young person in her twenties, and so when a new interpretation of *The Rite of Spring* choreographed by Yang Liping was included in the 2019 Melbourne International Arts Festival I attended eagerly with an artist friend, Aven Hodgess. We delighted in the panorama, the spectacle, the strangeness, the color of this magnificent production. In some ways it was a shame that the performance so closely antedated the global Covid-19 pandemic and that pandemic imagery colors at least some of the poem. But – Liping's interpretation brought a new spirituality to the ballet, a shift in perception from earthly, harvest, pagan, stomping "possession" to a mindfulness that I have continued to think about over the ensuing years. The concept of time as infinite, circular, is particularly present in the poem, in its form, as is a sense of space. Benevolence was not part of the original ballet. The intent is less to shock or shake things up than to provide solace in the face of inevitability.

Alvin Pang

National Gallery, I

Supremely comely forms court newcomers to the realm (discounts for teachers and frequent flyers) through skyscraping hallways echoey as, and emptied of, history's clutter, roofed and air-conditioned now, undusted (mostly: there are some corners and the lees of windows), returned to stateliness. Even the paintings look freshly 3D-printed, as if no hands sullied with chore and sweat ever fashioned them; the names of their creators austerely algorithmic, washed clean of life in gallery lighting and bland descriptors handwringingly ambivalent (because it's art mah, it's subjecteeth!), reflects this, engagement with that, diverse here and there, possibly, important, instability, change. Spit it out, man, what consciousness? The Galeri Nasional Indonesia had Raden Salleh casting glarefire at Dutch contempt, arresting submission; flagged warring factions of canvas and brush, testing the frame of things. But at least we have the acreage, the Michelin stars, the commanding view of the Padang, Smoke and Mirrors. As we turn our backs to look at horizon. At the rising and rising new, in the comfort of forgetting.

Commentary

'National Gallery, I' is part of an ongoing series of prose poems to do with particular places in my home city of Singapore. Cities are accretions of memory and affect in both broadly public and intensely personal ways; they are artifacts of design and confluences of sensory experiences that are the outcome of many interventions, crafted or unintended, over time. My series, including this piece, engages with this amalgamation of information, impression and significance, in which the individual perspective is but one of many layers of encounter and reading: one of a multitude of brushstrokes, yet nevertheless present, part of the composite of place.

In writing these prose poems, I add my stream of reflections and observations alongside and interweaving with other voices and views, some of which I derive from archival research or popular media. I mean for the unbroken lines of prose poetry to suggest these intertwined flows of meaning; to encompass without predetermining the myriad different ways the lines might be broken and segmented, the meanings framed.

This particular piece was written in late 2022, while I was part of a WrICE writers' residency which had been granted a working space for the week in the foyer of Singapore's National Gallery. On our second day, as a creative provocation, we writers-in-residence – hailing from various communities in Southeast Asia and Australia, thought to browse the Gallery's collection and then to freely write afterwards, with no explicit expectation to respond to the collection. But many of us did.

Fashioned by combining and refurbishing two colonial era institutions – the Supreme Court and City Hall – the

National Gallery Singapore (NGS), was launched in 2015 to much fanfare, as the world's largest public collection of modern Southeast Asian Art. The Gallery's approach to representing the regional artistic canon has been critiqued by observers such as Bharti Lalwani ('Singapore's New National Gallery Dubiously Rewrites Southeast Asian Art History', *Hyperallergic*, 1 Feb 2016)[1] as lacking in the socio-political context necessary to do justice to the turbulent, often contentious, modern history that has shaped the region's rich art heritage.

Browsing the National Gallery again after having recently visited the smaller but much more critically and contextually engaged Galeri Nasional Indonesia in Jakarta, I found the NGS's framing of its collection disingenuously banal, too safely generalised, too anxious to avoid contention or offence, keener that the NGS be seen as an architectural showcase and tourist destination than as an incisive or even informative contribution to thinking about SE Asian art. Hence, I drafted my poem as an ekphrasis of an ekphrasis: an immediate, impressionistic, impulsively journaled (and irritated) reaction to the coiffured and confected picture that the NGS as institution and as place has painted of SE Asian art and history. I numbered the piece 'I' as a gesture to the naming convention of many modern art pieces, but also fully intending to write further responses later. I have since let the piece stand alone, with the title suggesting that this is but one of many possible viewpoints at play, elsewhere or to come.

---

1. https://hyperallergic.com/271919/singapores-new-national-gallery-dubiously-rewrites-southeast-asian-art-history/

ANNE CALDWELL

Emily's Ghost

after a painting by Paola Suh Folicadi

i.

Because he is gone so long
hope is no longer a thing   with feathers
at first no telegram   no letter
I am clinker built and full of fortitude
so I hold the family together   a safe berth

> *and now there came both mist and snow*
> *and it grew wondrous cold*
> *and ice mast high   came floating by*
> *as green as emerald*

ii.

The ship is held in ice like a fist
I know that much   dream of the creak
and groan   crack and growl
hold my breath for five   blank months

loneliness is a tightness
in the oesophagus   I am
a ship's mast that senses
    my husband will surely find a way
    to bring the men home

Perce Blackborow   storekeeper
Frank Worsley   captain
John Vincent   sailor
Thomas Crean   second officer
Huberht Hudson   navigator

iii.

today I am a peregrine
sitting on her nest   I have a clutch
of speckled eggs that need turning
I long   for my mate
to do the night shift

She's going boys, she's going boys
Ernest shouts when the ship sinks
I cannot imagine   the colour that appears
just as the Weddell sea turns from   water into ice
aquamarine maybe   or a petrol oily blue

iv.

he tells me that in the *darkening twilight*
a lone star hovers   gem like above the bay
and how he yearns for me   it was my money
that sent him into a frozen wasteland
beyond love   away on his madcap adventure

Commentary

Ekphrasis as a process is a familiar one to me and has been a feature of my writing practice for many years. I often start writing with another media in mind and have spent time in art galleries, particularly The Tate and Leeds City Art Gallery, soaking up the stimulus that they provide. In this instance, I began by looking at a digital image of a painting on my laptop. The work was a striking picture of the *Endurance*, Shackleton's ship, which was stuck in the ice in 1915. It was by a female artist, Paola Suh Folicadi, and was painted on three separate panels of artificial suede. When exhibited, these panels hung together from the ceiling, giving an illusion of movement. It was not available for public display but immediately caught my attention. I challenged myself to look closely and try to imagine texture and color. I considered whether it made a difference that I was not physically present in the same room as the painting. I do think that working from a digital image had benefits in this particular creative process. Ekphrasis uses art as a starting point and often comes to life when a writer moves away from the media that inspires, into their own emotional and intellectual responses. I achieved this more quickly because I had to fill in the gaps in my mind of what this painting of the ship might feel like and its color palette. I wrote quickly, without too much research getting in the way of a first draft. I found a voice for the writing that suited Shackleton's wife, Emily. This idea of a persona and a dramatic monologue gave me a way into a hidden narrative behind the image of the famous ship, and the familiar story of Shackleton's saving of his crew. Seeing the events through Emily's eyes brought into view the perspective of those who are 'left behind' in an expedition: in this case, Shackleton's wife (and wives of soldiers of the First World War), and his crew members.

Paola Suh Folicadi had immersed herself in reading Shackleton's diaries and other material about the expedition and evidently went slightly crazy after months of painting the subject matter. I was hoping not to do the same! She found it difficult to return to everyday life. I also turned to the diaries and further research about Emily's life as a way of adding textures to my writing, as well as looking at the original black and white photographs of the ship and the crew. I reflected on the fact that I had written before about shipwrecks, particularly the HMS *Terror* (Franklin's ship in the Arctic), and am fascinated with the poetic nature of a ship being found again after such a time lapse. The HMS *Terror* was found in 2016 and the *Endurance* was discovered in the Weddell Sea in 2022. They are both now protected marine monuments. Could this fascination with a ship's discovery mirror a creative process? Was I diving down, Adrienne Rich style, to explore the idea of a wreck? Just as I had to fill in some of the gaps in appreciating Folicadi's artwork, my poem lent itself to a form on the page without punctuation, and I then experimented with the use of spatial caesura. I used the white space to represent the idea of pack ice, and an imaginative sense of a landscape that I wanted to be present in the background of the text itself. Like Folicadi, I have never been to Antarctica. I don't see the continent completely without colour but imagine it as shades of blue, as a last surviving remnant of wilderness. This project has been a very fruitful process for me and I have enjoyed experiments in shape and layout, after writing purely prose poetry for the last year. I am now considering using Folicadi's other paintings as the starting point for a poetic sequence based on the Shackletons and the infamous voyage.

JANÉE J. BAUGHER

Andrew Wyeth's Footnotes to *Distant Thunder,* 1961

1. "Some say the world will end in fire, / Some say in ice." (Frost)
2. *Realist Painter.*
   * Paint what's absent.
   † Voyeur collector.
   ‡ Composite portraits.
   § Allegiance to no one.
3. Beyond the meadow, on the forest floor, new ferns.
4. Daisies spring up, enliven white the straw-colored meadow.
5. Before I knew it, Betsy had walked out with our Labrador, dry grass under her shoes, the sky above blithe-light.
6. When I see her next, she's lying in the grass.
7. Legs in beige pants, ankles crossed. Blue blouse buttoned-up, arms folded over her torso.
8. She drops the floppy hat over her face.
9. Perched near the evergreens, Rattler will not dart off.
10. The binoculars beside her resting body.
11. Blueberry-brimming wooden crate and mug.
12. When I approach, Rattler doesn't stir.
13. I am unsurprised to see her supine: predictably full from berries flung up and mouth-caught.
14. When, in the distance, a clap of thunder, she stirs.
15. She rises. Hesitates.
16. I dread being seen.
17. *Betsy doesn't have to give a shit about me.*
18. She hangs the binoculars around her neck, grabs the berries, and follows Rattler out.

19. Finally, alone with my half-worked sketch.
20. "I turned ... to the woods, where I was better known."
(Thoreau)

2. † Knutson, Anne Classen, et al. *Andrew Wyeth: Memory and Magic*. 2nd ed., Rizzoli, 2006, (p. 73).

16. Meryman, Richard. *Andrew Wyeth: A Secret Life*. HarperCollins, 1998, (p. 175).

17. Meryman, Richard. *Andrew Wyeth: A Secret Life*. HarperCollins, 1998, (p. 148).

Previously published: *Green Mountains Review* (31), Vermont, Feb. 2020

Commentary

"Andrew Wyeth's Footnotes to *Distant Thunder,* 1961" is one poem from my newly completed full-length manuscript of researched, fictional-autobiographical musings to the artwork of American painter Andrew Wyeth (1917–2009), *The Andrew Wyeth Chronicles.* Each poem takes the form of footnotes, which seemingly charts his artistic process. Furthermore, someone viewing his artwork could reference these footnotes, which read as if Wyeth himself is providing commentary.

While in Sitka, Alaska, for a nonfiction writing fellowship in April 2012, I also participated in National Poetry Writing Month by doing daily freewrites. After having visited the Pennsylvania Art Museum in 2006, where I fell in love with Wyeth's paintings, a friend gifted me the artbook, *Andrew Wyeth: Memory & Magic* (Knutson). Somewhere I read that Wyeth was most productive when he felt "disembodied and invisible," feelings I could relate to. His muted color palettes, interest in the natural world, and illustrations of realism and abstraction inspired me. So, with that book and prompts from www.napowrimo.net, by the month's end I had completed 45 freewrites.

By June 2013 I had drafts of 80 poems, but the project came to a screeching halt when I shifted my attention to other manuscripts. By November of 2017, though, because my local museum had featured an Andrew Wyeth retrospective, my interest bloomed again. In my notebook, I began to draft ideas for the manuscript. On January 3, 2018, my notions for structure included "heteronyms in the vein of Fernando Pessoa, flash fiction, sestinas, prose poems, ekphrastic poems, monologues, or fictional biography."

On January 22nd I wondered if I could "Create a new genre or use a hybrid genre of ekphrastic fictional autobiography wherein I can imagine his creative process?" I had read online in an excerpt of Richard Meryman's manuscript, "Andrew Wyeth: A Secret Life," that Wyeth's "work often contains fragments." I conjectured that he fragmented himself from life in order to make his art whole.

Then, on January 31st, in large letters overtaking the entire page, I wrote, "Deconstructed poems!" On the next page: "deconstructed ekphrastic poems—hybrid—cross-genre— historical biography—fragmented ekphrastic musings—cliff notes, end notes, footnotes—What symbols? [1, 2] * † etc." I thought back to a random note I'd made in 2007 about wanting to use the paragraph symbol (¶) in a poem.

On February 8th I had obtained the Meryman book, which would be the first of 30 references I'd use. According to that source, Wyeth said some curious things: "I have this hate within me" (p. 5) and "Sometimes I think I'm not very artistic" (p. 7). Within just the first seven pages of Meryman's book, my synapses were firing in all sorts of creative directions.

By February 18th I had worked out the manuscript's chronology, whereby I'd "use the paintings' dates so as to create a foundation for a narrative progression." Additionally, I had decided to "research books that are footnote or endnote laden," and I had settled on each poem's point-of-view when I wondered, "Third person point-of-view? Wait. Actually, it should be in first person. As he paints he also keeps notebooks (I imagine) in which he commits his thoughts about art and life."

In the end, I used three types of references: Wyeth's artwork for influence, references to provide content for the narratives, and references for structure. For the latter, I embarked on a survey of literary styles: I studied *The Chicago Manual of Style*, I studied the artistic uses of footnotes in literature (e.g. Garrison Keillor's *Lake Wobegon Days*, David Foster Wallace's *Infinite Jest*, John Green's *An Abundance of Katherines*, Mark Dunn's *Ibid: A Life: A Novel in Footnotes*), and I read *American Hybrid: A Norton Anthology of New Poetry*.

I dove into Wyeth biographies for fodder, for I knew that if I could unearth just a few seeds, I could start to grow my poems. For example, it interested me that Frost and Thoreau were among his favorite writers and that his father was a renowned illustrator. The landscape of Chadds Ford, Pennsylvania and Cushing, Maine, and tidbits on his family and friends also offered me portals in. Learning that after his canvases were completed, his wife (Betsy) assigned titles to them was crucial. As a longtime ekphrastic writer who has relished leaning on information provided by artworks' titles, for this project I could virtually ignore his.

Given "Andrew Wyeth's Footnotes to *Distant Thunder,* 1961," to designate it as a poem is perhaps problematic. No line breaks exist, sound isn't the driving element, and the sentences are prosaic. Though, while I wasn't conscious of it, I can see now that all seven modes of imagery are present. Quotes are used, Frost (first line) and Thoreau (last line) and Wyeth (line 17), as well as biographical facts, such as the models were his wife and Rattler the Labrador. In line two, with the term "realist painter" and its list of definitions, I got to employ symbols. If there were a fifth definition, you'd see the ¶ symbol. One thing's for sure: my verbal description of his painting *Distant Thunder* does render the work "ekphrastic" in the etymological sense of the word.

Lisa Matthews

Lubiana Laibach

Scree line fury-held bound for landfall; over sea salt and basalt to forest floor. Now antler of snow and sleet, braided haunch and high to hind, the pelt of a boy alone in a landscape.

Listen for the crack of knees, the iron-hard ground, the impact as the rabbit in the garden falls – it fell, and it is always about to fall – out of the wooden cage onto the drain cover years below. Wire-kissed, a leaf-frozen curl at the corner of its mouth as doe eyes close in the garden where we spent so many Wednesday afternoons.

A crown of broken willow branches awaits his return. The path so dark, no fellow traveller by his side. He who was went away, has gone his way and lived to see another day, another tenner spent on White Lightening and Lambert & Butler Lites. His wintered shoulders and ice-burned hooves, knife in pocket, numbers for a shelter and the food bank.

The gyre-call catches on the wind, he waits to wonder then begins the slow walk down to the town by the sea, that is edged with trees and is both inland and out. He knew, he knows and will always know I chose to stay here with my other who he warmed to and welcomed. Body, eye, and ear adapt with the ink-dark bark, the ink-dark bark, which he coughs from his throat in the --ack --ack --ack I learned to make out at the edge of platforms, and quaysides, and central reservations of busy motorways. In stairwells and hostels. From the other side of A&E curtains.

And then. Just like that. We are new. And we are here. In this room, in an upper flat, in a house in another seaside town, the name of which I still cannot say. His outline fills the doorway, his legs unsteady on the carpeted floor. The muscles of his neck shift as he moves his head to the side, to get his antlers through.

The man with one leg has left to score, his wife sleeping in the room next door. The television on, something starting as the credits roll, a white cat sleeping on a back-yard wall.

Nothing is said. He walks to me, bends his knees, and gives his weight to the floor, where I feel I have been waiting – perhaps since he left – for this day. His breath shallows, he lays his head in my lap. I am cross-legged, it could be any year, anywhere. He doesn't look at me, just rests and the sweat on his neck seeps through the trousers I am wearing and goes cold.

His neck moulds across my legs, head softening in to angles we both know to be death. We let it in. It floods the room, is warm like tar. I feel his breath slow to stop, and so his heart. And so, this hart. My hand covers his eyes, the other warms his side as I sing that song we sang when he was born:

Our Daniel he's a funny 'un, he's got a nose like a pickled onion, a face like an angel, and eyes like two stars.

Commentary

'Lubiana Laibach' is a *present text* prose poem written in response to the film of the same name by UK filmmaker and critic Michael Pattison. It is also a creative exploration and expression of my complex grief, and a way to tackle challenging themes with my writing practice. Themes specifically associated with complex bereavement disorder and familial estrangement.

The *present text*, a consequence of ekphrastic writing activities, is at the heart of my doctoral research into sequential prose poems and their potential to help transform life experience into writing practice. The main characteristics of *present text* poems include:

+ They are written in planned, single and continuous writing sessions.

+ After the poems are written they are not edited, instead they remain in their original emergent form.

+ The only editorial alterations, when necessary, are to ensure consistency of viewpoint and tense.

+ The intent of present texts is that they remain un-edited but occupy the page in the state in which they emerged.

+ Present texts emerge in response to pre-determined constraints set up around an artwork, or artworks.

+ Most importantly present texts have a momentum borne from the sequential nature of the stimuli they emerge in response to. In this case Pattison's film which is a sequential filmic meditation of place, that focuses on sculptural objects in the landscape.

+ It is the momentum and sequentiality of the film that affects and shapes the present text it informs.

Why call 'Lubiana Laibach' a *present text?* Why not a draft, or a piece of automatic writing, a sketch, a maquette, or notes towards a new poem? The answer lies, in the case of my own practice, in the fact that *present texts* are a way to explore things too traumatic to hold. In this instance the death of my nephew. This is the core of my practice-led doctoral research.

The poem shared here is taken from my forthcoming collection of prose poems, *The hauled-up notebooks* (due for UK publication, by Red Squirrel Press, in autumn 2024).

The theoretical aspects of a *present text* are explored in depth in my thesis. Here, I will share the specific set up for 'Lubiana Laibach'. When I planned the poem, I knew I wanted to explore testimony I witnessed at the inquest into the death of my nephew. Since attending the inquest, during which I took notes so I would have a record of what the Coroner said, I have wanted to honor my nephew. At the end of his life, he was sitting on the floor, where he had been put by friends, surrounded by cushions to prop him up. He sat down and died. I couldn't hold this reality in my mind, so I decided, when the time was right, to create something artistic from the horror of the reality. 'Lubiana Laibach' is what emerged.

When I first saw it at a PGR Conference in Hospitalfield in Scotland, Pattinson's first film, *Lea Valley Bridges*, moved me to tears. At the time I had no idea why. It was something to do with the quiet humanity knitted together into the static, yet still moving, images of boats and canal paths and random strangers walking past. The narrative of this film was the river itself and where Pattinson decided to place his camera, at every bridge over the River Lea.

When I heard Pattinson had made another film, I knew immediately that I wanted to use it in a *present text* set-up.

The poem here is the product of a 3-hour auto-performance and micro-residency at the Newcastle (upon Tyne) gallery space, Baltic 39. With agreement and facilitation from curators, I occupied a small, windowless gallery room where I had access to a large screen TV and the ability to work completely in the dark. Signage was put up around the gallery, so people knew not to interrupt me. I played Pattinson's film on a loop at least 3 times. At first, nothing happened. Then as I started to be drawn into the sequentiality of the film I began to write, almost as if in a trance. Typing straight into Word, in the light thrown from the television screen, the prose poem you read here is what came out. At the end of the *present text* activities, I was sitting on the floor, imagining my nephew's head in my lap as he died.

It sounds strange when I write it here. But that's what happened. I ended up on the floor, crying, exorcising something. I don't know what. Pain. Grief. Elation at the calm at the centre of this ekphrastic writing experience. In the future I plan to use *present text* set-ups for themes that are less traumatic, and less personal. For now, I feel the stag in the poems, the boy with the antlers, has found his place in a kinder, poetic place.

Mags Webster

La charmeuse de serpents

after La charmeuse de serpents *(1907) by Henri Rousseau, and*
"Yadwigha, on a Red Couch, Among Lilies: A Sestina for the
Douanier" (1958) by Sylvia Plath

This jungle knows how close to it she comes,
the tangled edge, its pointed lick of leaves.
She does not know where it begins and ends
or whether she can tame it, yet
the moon has broken free of clouds. *Another*
suffocating night is brewing in my head.

Faint starlight filters through the branches overhead.
How soon until the lacquered serpents come
plaiting the arsenic grass, one coupling with the other?
A zoomorphic noose among the leaves,
their bodies fold about her neck, and yet
they are most gentle with their muscled ends.

The jungle presses in, its musky dream ascends
to permeate the labyrinths of her head,
trap her in the tropics of its darkness, yet
she does not want the noise of day to come
and pierce her: sunlight's fanfare leaves
such naked scars. She needs another

kill to sate her blood, the ebbing of another's
throat to spool out from her flute. It often ends
this way: the green-breathed toxins of the leaves
start pulsing vapours in her head,
they blacken through her veins until they overcome
her – but – *I'll outwit this poison yet.*

She has the flute – the vatic instrument – yet
it's mute and rigid in her hands; another's
mouth may claim it. The snakes become
umbilical, they plug their sinuous ends
into placental night; a diamond head
weaves hieratic loops among the leaves

and suddenly, she lands her prey, cleaves
its being from its bones, a beast half-formed and yet
it satisfies the famish of her head.
She gorges on the rawness of the other,
feeds it to the flute, pretends
this music will not kill her, that its fatal spell is welcome.

Every dream leaves behind a stain. The other
night, I could not sleep (again). Nothing ends
this headache.
       I have a vision of the poems I would write, but do not.
When will they come?[1]

---

1. This line comes from Sylvia Plath's journal entry Sunday March 29, 1959.

Commentary

A Spell of Writing

A Rousseau poem: a green-leaved world ... the naked lady on her
red velvet couch in the jungle's middle: how close to this I come ...
this queer sickish greeny-vinous fatigue ... my life is a discipline,
a prison: I live for my own work, without which I am nothing.
My writing (Plath 2000, 347).

In 1957 Sylvia Plath (1932–63) began teaching at her alma
mater, Smith College in Massachusetts. She found lecturing
left no time or energy for her own work; her journal entry
(above) for 10 March 1958 expresses disenchantment and
frustration as she completes another exhausting semester.
After a fortnight's vacation, however, she writes to her mother
'I have at last burst into a spell of writing ... I've discovered
my deepest source of inspiration which is art' (Plath 2019,
222).

Alongside the work of DeChirico, Gauguin and Klee, Plath
is influenced by the canvases of Henri Julien Rousseau (1844–
1910). Under his sultry twilights of dense, fleshy foliage,
elaborate tableaux play out. The big cat's kill in *Le lion, ayant
faim, se jette sur l'antilope* (1898/1905); hypnotized snakes
uncoiling from their camouflage of leaves in *La charmeuse de
serpents* (1907); the surreal imagery of a woman on a couch,
surrounded by snakes, jaguars and a mysterious piper in *Le rêve*
(1910). These last two paintings seem to be the inspirations,
respectively, for Plath's poems 'Snakecharmer' (1957) and
'Yadwigha, on a Red Couch, Among Lilies: A Sestina for The
Douanier' (1958).

My poem draws from a painting and a poem. In terms of form, it responds to Plath's first and, as far as I know, only sestina. *La charmeuse de serpents*, however, furnishes the source material. On the edge of the jungle, a tranquil lagoon shimmers under the full moon. In the foreground stands a woman, eyes engaging directly with the viewer. She is clothed only in her own long hair, or maybe an animal skin. Moonlight silvers the curves of her legs. A snake around her neck, a flute held to her lips. Snake silhouettes rearing up from the grass, disengaging from trees.

It seems this painting is significant to Plath long before she writes her poetic response to it. In February 1956 she meets her future husband, Ted Hughes, and on their second encounter a month later, they spend a 'sleepless holocaust night' (Plath 2000, 552) together before Plath departs for Europe. On April 5 in Paris, she journals: 'I shall send [Ted] the postcard of Rousseau's *Snakecharmer* with a question. One night is not enough' (Plath 2000, 565). Here, the painting lures Plath and Hughes closer to the extraordinarily creative, sexual and ultimately destructive partnership they share. However, given Plath's 1958 journal declaration, the more meaningful and definitive relationship is arguably her lifelong one with her writing. Rousseau's painting thus becomes an erotically charged allegory of a poet's 'libido towards language' (Lewis in Preston 2013), and it is this that animates my sestina.

The patterned lexical repetition of a sestina's six line-ending words can evoke a sense of 'claustrophobic containment' (Preminger et al in Greene 2012, 1297). A build-up of pressure hints also at an intensifying drive towards some sort of release or satiation: perhaps of hunger, lust or intellect, or simply the palliative gift of sleep. Given the jungle setting, this desire could logically reach its apotheosis in the stalking and subduing of prey. But the issue of who – or what – is hunting who seems ambiguous. Is it the flute music? The 'other'? Is it the 'she' of the poem or the internalized 'I'? Or is it poetry itself?

Plath may have chosen the sestina form to mimic Rousseau's technique of painting each leaf and grass blade in a 'painted collage' (Büttner in Cluha et al 2010, 37). In April 1958, Lee Anderson interviewed Plath for the Library of Congress:

> Anderson asked her if it was "necessary to write in a strict form to get music." Plath answered:

> I like to work in forms that are strict, and yet the strictness isn't uncomfortable. Sort of like a comfortable corset or something, I suppose [laughs], that isn't really noticeable and obvious, but it's there ... I'm much happier when I know that all my sounds are echoing in different ways throughout the poem than if I just forget about it. (Clark 2022, 522)

Yet in the late 1950s Plath wrote often of wanting to break free of her 'too forced and rhetorical' (Plath 2000, 477) style. When one has been as assiduous a student of form and prosody as Plath, what does it take to reject the heft of poetic conventions and scholarship and instead strip the being from the bone? As later poems show, Plath didn't need the corset of form for her sounds to ring out in some of the most extraordinary free verse known to the English tongue. She had found her music.

Works Cited or Consulted:

Clark, H. 2022. *Red Comet: The Short Life and Blazing Art of Sylvia Plath*. London: Vintage.

Greene, R.S., C. Cushman, J. Cavanagh, J. Ramazani, and P. Rouzer, eds. 2012. *The Princeton Encyclopedia of Poetry & Poetics*. 4th edition. Princeton, New Jersey: Princeton University Press.

Plath, S. 2019. *The Letters of Sylvia Plath, Volume II: 1956–1963*. Paperback edition. Edited by Peter K. Steinberg and Karen V. Kukil. London: Faber and Faber.

Plath, S. 2000. *The Journals of Sylvia Plath*. Edited by Karen V. Kukil. London: Faber and Faber.

Plath, S. 1981. *Collected Poems*. London: Faber and Faber.

Preston, A. 2013. "Does Prozac help artists be creative?" *The Observer.* Sunday 19 May. Available at https://www.theguardian.com/culture/2013/may/19/does-prozac-help-artists-be-creative

—*Henri Rousseau.* 2010. Edited by D. Cluha, V. Locatelli, O. Strasser for Beyeler Museum. Ostfildern, Germany: Hatje Cantz Verlag.

Edwin Stockdale

The Afterlives of Edward II

They call me sodomite. Even now, in this age of tolerance, slurs are levied against me: *sexual proclivities with other men* or they erase my relationship with Piers as *brothers by blood. This would allow for a strong emotional tie, but also rule out a physical sexual relationship.* Best of all, when I got my wife pregnant, they say *at long last he played the man.* Now don't get me wrong, some have accepted me: *my identity has been inevitably affected by heteronormativity, and by the characterization of relationships between men as sensational and deviant.*

And I thank Christopher Marlowe for keeping my story alive and making it clear that my relationship with Piers was sexual and intimate. Says Piers: *the king, upon whose bosom let me die.* Later, I reply: *thy worth, sweet friend, is far above my gifts; therefore to equal it, receive my heart.* Kit Marlowe underlines Piers as my boyfriend: *like Leander, gasped upon the sand.* Make-up based on an effigy of my tomb at Gloucester Cathedral. *Sometime a lovely boy in Dian's shape.* In an open-air theatre Renaissance clothing, fur and steel. *And there hard by, one like Actaeon peeping through the grove.* That searing kiss, the first male-male kiss on British television. *For never doted Jupiter on Ganymede.* A middle-aged man's fascination with a pretty boy. *Great Alexander loved Hephestion.* Pert codpieces constantly at eye-level for the ground-floor audience. *The conquering Hercules for Hylas wept.* Non-binary actors play me. *He's gone, and for his absence thus I mourn.* I lie on top of Gaveston, erotic and tender, myself as flawed and deposed. *And now thy sight is sweeter far*

than was thy parting hence bitter and irksome to my sobbing heart.
I wear purple silk and lace, reach for his hand, caress his hairy
chest. *Embrace me Gaveston as I do thee.* He seduces me with
his hips, dark jeans, white t-shirt.

Derek Jarman's film *emphasizes the homoeroticism and the politics
of Marlowe's play, to demonstrate their crucial interconnection,
and to insist on their relevance to his and our contemporary world.*
My lover, leather-clad, bristles with sexual charisma and an
American accent, doubles as my executioner in the murder-by-
penetration scene. *And for Patroclus stern Achilles drooped.* A
candlelit indoor playhouse: I bid my final farewell to Perrot
from our separate galleries, the gulf of the stage between us as
we lean towards each other.

Commentary

My prose poem, as its title states, takes its inspiration from the afterlives of the bisexual medieval monarch, Edward II (1284–1327). I take ekphrasis in its traditional sense as the transfer of knowledge from one artform to another, rather than the more modern meaning of a poetic response to visual art. I decided that Edward would directly challenge what has been written about him by some historians. The phrase "sexual proclivities" with other men comes from an academic biography by Roy Martin Haines, whose language of proclivities suggests negativity and can be interpreted as biphobic.[1] The ruling out of a 'physical sexual relationship' between Edward and Piers Gaveston is a reference to the historian, Professor Seymour Phillips.[2] In Phillips's biography of Edward, part of the Yale English Monarchs series published by Yale University Press, he refers to Edward and Piers as sworn brothers and shuts down a discussion of Edward's sexuality. 'At long last he played the man' is an extraordinary comment by Alison Weir in her biography of Isabella, Edward's wife.[3] Even if ironic, Weir's phrasing is deeply unpleasant, and, even more shockingly, Weir's book was published as recently as 2005. The final sentence of the first paragraph-stanza, acknowledges that Edward is very satisfied with queer activist Kit Heyam's book about him: 'It is important to state explicitly that the historiography of Edward

---

1. Roy Martin Haines, *King Edward II: His Life, His Reign, and its Aftermath, 1284–1330* (McGill-Queen's University Press, 2003), p. 43.
2. Seymour Phillips, *Edward II* (Yale University Press, 2010), p. 103.
3. Alison Weir, *Isabella: She-Wolf of France, Queen of England* (Pimlico, 2005), p. 62.

II has been inevitably affected by heteronormativity, and by the characterization of relationships between men as sensational and deviant.[4]

The second verse-paragraph of my prose poem goes beyond texts written about Edward II by historians and takes in the Renaissance playwright Christopher Marlowe's *Edward II* (1594), and various stage productions of Marlowe's play throughout the twentieth and twenty-first centuries. The sentences in italics are mostly quotes from Marlowe's play and the images highlight how Marlowe's language makes it clear that Edward and Piers's relationship was intimate and sexual. On 30 October 1947, a production of Marlowe's play was transmitted by BBC television. The make-up of David Markham as Edward reflected his effigy at Gloucester Cathedral. The 'open-air theatre' is a reference to the Cambridge University Marlowe Society 1958 production at Stratford-upon-Avon where Derek Jacobi played Edward. It was also broadcast by the BBC Third Programme (now BBC Radio 3) on 1 March 1959. 'That searing kiss' was the passionate embrace by Ian McKellen and James Laurenson as Edward and Piers for the Edinburgh Festival in 1969, which was so successful it went on a national tour and had two spells in the West End at the Mermaid and Piccadilly theatres. When the production was broadcast on BBC Two the following year on 6 August 1970, it was the first time that a male-male kiss had been seen on British television. In 1986 Ian McDiarmid played the title role to Michael Grandage's Piers at the Royal Exchange, Manchester with an age difference of eighteen years between them, hence my line: 'A middle-aged man's fascination with a pretty boy.' 'Pert codpieces' refers to the Royal Shakespeare Company's 1990 production at the Swan Theatre with Simon Russell Beale as Edward and Grant Thatcher as Piers. In 1995 Eddie Izzard played Edward

---

4. Kit Heyam, *The Reputation of Edward II, 1305–1697: A Literary Transformation of History* (Amsterdam University Press, 2020), p. 19.

at the Leicester Haymarket, thus 'non-binary actors have played me'. When Joseph Fiennes and James D'Arcy played Edward and Piers in 2001 at the Sheffield Crucible, they lay on top of each other on the stage.'I wear purple silk and lace, reach for his hand, caress his hairy chest'. This alludes to the 2003 production at Shakespeare's Globe, where Liam Brennan and Gerald Kyd took on the roles of Edward and Piers.'He seduces me with his hips, dark jeans, white t-shirt' references Samuel Collings as Piers and Chris New as Edward in the modern-dress production at the Royal Exchange, Manchester in 2011.

Derek Jarman's 1991 film of Marlowe's play begins the final verse-paragraph. The text in italics is Stephen Guy-Bray's introduction to the New Mermaids edition: 'Jarman's greatest achievement was to emphasize the homoeroticism and the politics of the play, to demonstrate their crucial interconnection, and to insist on their relevance to his and our contemporary world'.[5] In 2013 at the National Theatre, Piers was played as an American in a leather jacket by Kyle Soller to John Heffernan's Edward: 'My lover, leather-clad, bristles with sexual charisma and an American accent, doubles as my executioner in the murder-by-penetration scene'. Finally, the "candlelit indoor playhouse" makes reference to the 2019 production at the Sam Wanamaker Playhouse at Shakespeare's Globe, a stage which is wood-paneled in the Jacobean style, where Tom Stuart and Beru Tessema played Edward and Piers. As can be seen in my prose poem, in addition to historical biographies of Edward II, I consulted Marlowe's play, Jarman's film, plus stills, reviews and recordings of various stage productions for my multilayered ekphrastic response.

---

5. Stephen Guy-Bray, 'Introduction,' in Christopher Marlowe, *Edward II*, eds. Martin Wiggins and Robert Lindsey, intr. Stephen Guy-Bray, New Mermaids (Methuen Drama, 2014), p. vii-xxxiv, p. xii.

FELICITY PLUNKETT

Life with Ghosts

after Olive Cotton's Windflowers, *with a line from Yi Lei*

Light gives and takes. *Make me a ghost,* draw into shade
what we've lost. In hintershade
petals fly up and light falls –
               nightfall's
trick – to change light into dust. Husked, we come apart, lie
fallow after summer. Call it the end. Part truth, part lie.
For months I could only look
at flowers at night, slip a lonely look
at lit night windows. I thought
of the way the moonflower opens for no one, thought
of distant friends who walked out pain,
wind picking off what loosened. Jamb, sash, pane,
cold butter light. To walk in a body no one knows. Rose ghost.
Each time one of us leaves the other, rogue ghosts
move close, roll shadows across the walls of lovedark
rooms. Host us. And at the end of love, dark
folds, wakes, packs its case. We live with ghosts –
ghosts of water running from pipes above, ghosts'
prints where flame scorched wood, hair in the teeth
of a comb, your smile in photos all glint and dogteeth.
               To give equal weight to light
and shade, to weigh on invisible scales what can't be held. To light
absence. I can't quite hear what she says, your love
who died, but she tells me it's alright. Love,
in your hand is an offer
and it's alright. I can never be the ghost of her.

Commentary

Olive Cotton's *Experimental Windflower Montage With Shadow Pattern* is a gelatin silver photograph on paper. A montage of two negatives, it is a variant of her famous photograph *Windflowers* (c.1939). I love its ghostliness and sense of movement.

A few years ago, after a bereavement, I developed the habit of walking at night, either with one of my children, a friend, or alone. The intimacy and quiet power of Cotton's image evokes for me the experience of being outside at night, with the sense of others' lives taking place beyond lit windows, and the presence of flowers, sometimes barely visible, spectral.

Thinking about how to write a poem in response to this photograph, I started with an intuitive sense of connection to its spirit and mood. It reminded me of a phrase from Chinese poet Yi Lei's 'A Single Woman's Bedroom' (1986)[1] – 'make me a ghost'—a line I find exhilarating, connected as it is with another image: 'She belongs to no-one, / sitting like a ghost beyond her own reach'. Layered with the poem's loss is a powerful sense of endurance. Although the poem's pulse is the refrain 'You didn't come to live with me', it is a poem about solitude's expansiveness, and freedom: a woman's freedom from the tyrannous position of object, now seen only by her own eyes, and the individual's freedom from unjust restrictions. Yi Lei drafted the poem's 240 lines in a night. Published to acclaim, the poem was later denounced by conservative critics in China.

The poem is a reclamation of desire and agency, and at its heart is the woman alone. The version I know is a translation

1. Lei, Yi. *My Name Will Grow Wide Like a Tree*. Translated by Tracy K. Smith and Changtai Bi, Graywolf Press, 2020.

by Tracy K. Smith (one of my favorite poets) and Changtai Bi. This is another kind of montage, this time of translators' complementary skills. Smith's description of her process guided me towards my own ekphrastic translation of Cotton's photograph, now layered in my mind with Yi Lei's poem. She writes: 'My strategy, whenever I reached a point of hesitation, was to ask the surrounding features of the poem to suggest a continuity that might guide me forward.' She aimed 'to cleave to the original spirit, tone, and impetus.'

Helen Ennis' meticulous work on Olive Cotton's life and work was another guide. Ennis' work also faced a restriction in terms of her subject's 'reserve, reticence and modesty'.[2] Reading letters from the two men who were Cotton's husbands, Ennis writes that Cotton 'flickers in and out of their writing as the one being addressed but never assumes a firm presence'. (5) This, and Cotton's description of photography as 'drawing with light' offered ways into my poem.

My first draft had a few phrases I heard, loosely connected. As the poem expanded, I wanted my poem's form to resonate with the sense of layering produced by Cotton's montage of negatives. I used echo verse to do this, in which the last sounds of each line are repeated in the next line, sometimes inexactly, as an echo. Edward Hirsch writes that 'the bodiless sense of missed connection haunts the tradition of echo poems'.[3]

Somewhere along the way, I realized my poem was about ghosts as well as echoes, and about the way that, when we lose someone, we continue a conversation they may or may not hear. The last words on Nick Cave and the Bad Seeds' album *Skeleton Tree*, an album shaped in the aftermath of the death of Cave's fifteen-year-old son Arthur, are: 'it's alright now, it's alright'. It feels as though this is something we might tell

---

2. Ennis, Helen. *Olive Cotton: a Life in Photography*. Fourth Estate, 2019, 5.
3. Hirsch, Edward. *The Essential Poet's Glossary*. Mariner, 2017, 85.

ourselves, whispered encouragement. The song "Skeleton Tree" starts with an image of someone calling out across the sea "but the echo comes back empty," yet it moves towards this tentative and consolatory echo.

Contesting Freud's idea of melancholia as a pathological perversion of mourning, Jacqueline Rose, writing about Virginia Woolf, asks: 'What is this love that, in mourning as opposed to melancholia, steadfastly, decidedly, works to extinguish itself'?[4] and 'What on earth does it mean to suggest that the living do not, should not, identify with the dead'? (77)

Love does not extinguish itself, and we live among the shades and shapes of those we have loved. 'Life With Ghosts' maps traces of the losses in the lives of lovers whose impressions move through the poem. The two negatives Cotton brought together create a restive conversation, like the layers of connection and echo ekphrastic work expresses; like the way solitude and intimacy are layered in our lives, like loss and gain.

Note:
> https://www.joseflebovicgallery.com/pages/books/CL178-52/olive-cotton-aust/experimental-windflower-montage-with-shadow-pattern

---

4. Rose, Jacqueline. *On Not Being Able to Sleep: Psychoanalysis and the Modern World.* Princeton UP, 2003, 76.

IAN SEED

Secondary Education

for Martin

It's the school cross-country, my first. Both
my feet are off the ground. There's Mr Hunt
in stripey scarf and bobble hat, cheering
me on, Mr Hunt my favourite teacher
who gives me A's for English, who my mum
says is dishy, though he's married and looks
happy. I wouldn't mind him for a dad.

I'm ahead of the other boys. How has that
happened? All I'm doing is running.
But in the mud by a gate, a plimsoll
comes off and my fingers are too frozen
to get it back on. With a bleeding foot
I finish eleventh out of more than a hundred –
I've found the only sport I'm good at.

I never get A's for RE, taught
by Mr Austin. He has Brylcreemed black hair
combed back in thin strands. He stinks
of cigarettes and my mum says she wouldn't
want him kissing her. He gets suspended
for touching up a girl, but he's back soon
and tells me off for picking my nose in class.

Commentary

Although I felt honored to receive the invitation to contribute to this anthology, I also felt paralyzed, as is often the case when I receive a commission, especially by the idea of writing a self-reflective commentary. I was also aware of the absurdity of my paralysis – hadn't I for the best part of the last two decades been asking my students to write this kind of self-criticism as a component of their portfolios submitted for assessment?

When it comes to producing ekphrastic work in the past, I have used paintings by Edward Hopper, Joseph Cornell, Giorgio de Chirico and others as starting points for both prose and verse poems of an abstract or surrealist nature.[1] This time I decided to use a black-and-white photograph of myself at the age of twelve running in a school cross-country race in 1968, and to challenge myself to write something more "realist" and autobiographical. "Life writing" I have always found difficult, even though I have taught it for several years. I worry that anything coming directly from my own life will be dull to read, reek of self-pity, and lose itself in details without any interesting narrative to shape them.

The odd thing was that I did not have the photo to hand, and so had to write from my memory of the photo. I began (instructing myself along the way, as if I were one of my own students) by writing a brief description of the photo (as I remembered it), and then making a list of all the associations that came to mind, which included memories of different

---

1. See, for example, 'Quieter than ever' in *Shifting Registers* (Shearsman, 2011), 'Late' in *New York Hotel* (Shearsman, 2018) and 'Night Window', in *Free Verse* 31, 2020, online: https://freeversethejournal.org/issue-31-2020-ian-seed/

teachers (good and bad), my parents' divorce, a family tragedy, a school fight I backed out of, friends and enemies, and my later adolescent rebellion. Again, I was getting lost in details, I was meant to be writing a shortish poem, not my own (terrible) version of *In Search of Lost Time*. A couple of days later, I returned to the photo itself, focusing on what I could see and what I most directly associated with it; other associated events would stay in the background, but still be a presence, for example my parents' bitter divorce.

I wrote initially in prose, and then, as I sometimes do when trying to cut down to what is essential, I rewrote the prose as blank verse. When I presented this early draft that same evening to my writers' group, they thought it was still quite loose and 'prosy'. I took their comments on board and made further cuts.[2] With this further reshaping, the poem revealed itself to be what I hope is both funny and quietly moving, giving the reader a snapshot of an English Secondary Modern school at that time, and of my life within that system, and also, I hope, reflecting some of the feelings and experiences most of us have at school.

But why that particular photo, I asked myself once the poem was written. Why not one of many others that I actually have to hand? The answer, I think, is that, without knowing it, I wanted to call on a sense of resilience in the face of adversity, especially as my mother (a key character in the poem) died quite recently, and I am of course feeling the effects.

More than half a century on, I still go running (or perhaps 'jogging' these days) to keep my spirits up and clear my mind. I especially like to go for solitary runs in the early morning when it is still dark and to keep going until the sun rises.

---

2. I also workshopped a revised copy with a group of first-year poetry students I was teaching at the University of Chester. I wanted to encourage them not to be afraid of bringing in 'shitty first drafts' of their own poems.

BOB HEMAN

Information

after Ensor

Without their flesh to keep them warm they must huddle closer
to the fire.

Commentary

I did not write this piece to be an ekphrastic poem. It was just another one of my "information" pieces, part of a series of short prose poems I've been adding to for over 20 years, prose poems that explore tiny microcosms in which all things are possible. The pieces work in a variety of ways, sometimes based on real experience, but more often than not a product of my imagination. Some are quite minimal, while others are more linear, frequently bouncing off of legends and fairy tales, or the conventions of genre films. Sometimes they resemble surrealism or list poems, and often play with language.

But although this was not intended to be an ekphrastic poem, it certainly is, inspired by and referencing James Ensor's 1889 painting *Skeletons Warming Themselves*, one of a series of paintings he did in which skeletons or masks play a prominent role.

I have always loved the portrayal of skeletons in art, including the *memento mori* and "Dance of Death" images created during the Renaissance, and the Day of the Dead prints of Mexican popular artist José Guadalupe Posada. That is one of the reasons why this painting particularly appealed to me.

It would be wrong to think that ekphrastic poems can only be written to "look like" traditional poetry. It is also quite possible for ekphrastic poems to be visual poems, or minimal poems, or even sound poetry. The room for experimentation is there, just as it is in any poem. There's no reason not to explore it.

NILOOFAR FANAIYAN

Voyage

It begins by the fountain, beneath the oculus –
stars at the edge of clouds eager to move. The hub cradles

the beginning and the middle – the water of life rises up,
from the Ocean of His Words are the tomes and codexes.

The sound of rushing water mingles
with the perfume of petrichor, weaves past fern-like leaves,
through glass, across marble, feeding the atmosphere,
swelling and ebbing around minds seeking, souls yearning.

Shafts of dawn-light stream through tall pillars, tracing
the half-circle, vibrating through ether, embracing
the seeker with the warmth of promise, and chasing
her steps as she enters through the glass doors.

The stream lights up at stations along the journey. It flows
        throughout
like veins and tributaries, welling up like sounds in a desert.
        They are
calling to each other,
        each word a drop
                and each drop an ocean
                        and each ocean a universe –

friends hoist the mast, one checks the coordinates,
others the rigging, another the direction of the wind. They all
    have their eyes on the horizon –

she was destined to step onto this ship.
She stands beneath the oculus, beside the fountain.

Commentary

Standing inside the Centre for the Study of the Texts in Haifa, Israel,[1] has always had a soothing effect on my mind and spirit while, at the same time, there is the subtle buzz of intense work being carried out quietly and diligently throughout the building. Internal courtyards, gardens and fountains create a unique quality of light at every point and on every level. The building is poetry incarnate, both in terms of its architecture and its purpose. The classically designed portico, which draws the observer inside and draws the insider outdoors, felt like the perfect setting for the beginning and ending of a narrative.

Ekphrasis, as a form of reading and mediating lived narrative, can be an immersive experience.[2] More than being a description or simple commentary, it is the expression of what emerges from your mind when you see potentialities and possibilities in a work of art, when you inhabit that work and it becomes the prompt and even the setting for exploring reality through a particular lens. In other words, you "read" the narrative that is inherent in the music/image/structure and mediate that narrative. Through this experience, you enter into a dialogue with another artist or creator. And beyond this dialogue, you become an artistic or creative collaborator in world building.

---

1. See http://www.amanatarchitect.com/cst/index.php for images and more information.

2. Monika Fludernik has pioneered, and written extensively on, the concept of experiential narratology. See Monika Fludernik. *Towards a 'Natural' Narratology* (London: Routledge, 1996).

Over the years I have found myself responding to art through exploring primarily two types of narrative: narratives regarding the creation of art, as in Jacquelin du Pre's performance of Elgar's Cello Concerto in E minor, and narratives that are evoked by a work of art, as in the case of *The Great Wave off Kanagawa* by Hokusai. In composing 'Voyage', I was responding to both types of narrative; the nature of the architecture and the narrative that it evokes, and the lived experience of spending time in the building and engaging with some of the concepts found in some of the texts that are studied in this center.

The composition process, similar to my writing of other ekphrastic poems, began when I was struck with the sensation of awe. For me, it always starts with wanting to spend more time with an artwork, whether I am listening to music, examining an image, or wandering through the different spaces within a building. I had been spending time with the Centre for the Study of the Texts for some years and waxing poetic about its structure and atmosphere when, finally, the opportunity arose to explore the space on a more literary level.

Throughout the first part of the process, as I jotted down notes and phrases and mulled over concepts while watching clouds pass through the oculus over the portico, I was aware that perhaps the architect and the people working in and around the environment might one day read this poem. In some ways, this created a restriction in my expression. However, it also challenged me to strive to honor the sacred nature of the building and the work carried out within. The narrative of the seeker and a collective voyage arose from the ever-present motifs of water, shifting light, and different spaces/levels.

Ultimately, the process of creating and decoding narrative is a process of reading, interpreting, and meaning making. It is the process that our minds are engaged in both on a micro level and on a macro level, in relation to moments and in relation to large blocks of timing, experience/s. 'Reading' this building is, for me, not a finite experience. Rather, it holds endless possibilities. While I have attempted to represent what I personally perceived as a moment of reality in 'Voyage', my hope is that other artists will also be inspired to respond to such spaces.

NATHAN LANGSTON

Early Sunday Morning, 1930, by Edward Hopper

You linger on Seventh Avenue almost a century ago,
gazing across the street at a 2-story row of shops and apartments.
The sun has recently risen over the Hudson to your right,
its warmth on your cheek, still so close to the horizon that the
      shadows
of street signs stretch out straight for full blocks.

The rough avenue cobblestones seem smooth in warm,
buttery light. Seventh Avenue is a Stonehenge.
The shadows run so perfectly leftward along the compass rose
of the street plan, that it feels meant to be.
It is early on Sunday morning, still
chilly on what will be a hot day.

Did you wake up before everyone or did you stay
up all night? Either way, there are no people here,
only you, and you are barely here either.
This quiet is not common.
New York City, empty of people,
overflows with ghosts.

Notice the darkened green doorways,
each recess a near-black rectangle. Notice
how your eyes can register painted signs
on every shop window but you can't make out

what they say. Notice white shutters
and yellow shades in the second story apartments,
pulled up and down in perfectly accidental patterns.
Notice the heartbreaking gradient of light blue
to lighter blue in the cloudless sky and the sharp
dark geometry of a large building in the distance.

Why did you stop here? Why have you looked so long?

Is it because the ruddy red of NY brownstone, all from the
      same quarries
in those early days, glows like the word of God at sunrise and
      sunset?
Maybe it's that little fire hydrant, somehow stately in the dawn.
Is it that the old barbershop pole might be slightly crooked to
      the left
and you tilt your head back and forth, wondering if it's off kilter
      or you are?

Or did you glimpse a scene as empty
and as hallowed as yourself,
finding some comfort in the sight?

A century later, I stand at the exact spot
and at the very hour. A strange, holy
radiance graces the ramshackle surfaces
of all this sad human brick and draws
this broke city into the curvature of Earth.

I wonder about you, standing there, looking.
There is such a slight, vital difference
between *lonely* and *alone*.

Commentary

By selecting this Edward Hopper painting, I opted to include something deeply New York City and American in the collection of works. Painting at a time when Abstract Expressionism was in vogue, Hopper hewed toward the traditions of folks like Norman Rockwell and Andrew Wyeth, in which narrative and poetry rises to the fore. The cleanliness of his architectural aesthetics, realism and use of light and color, lends itself easily to the ekphrastic translation of images into words.

For a salon here in Seattle, I recently interviewed a person whose job it was to create linguistic descriptions of visual works for non-sighted visitors to museums. His recommendation was to abide by the old advice of "say what you see," but also suggested another rule, "don't say what you don't see." If the point of ekphrasis is direct translation to folks who can't see it, get out of the way and don't add in your impressions and associations. That interpretation is the job of the audience, not you. As a describer, you're just a telescope or microscope, making visible what is invisible, and it's the job of the listeners or readers to make up their own minds about what the subject means.

Compared to my curator and art critic friends, I'm rubbish at pure formal analysis. But that strategy stands in contrast to how ekphrasis was originally practiced in ancient Greece. It wasn't just formal analysis but "giving voice to" a work so that you felt as though it was speaking directly to you. In Hopper's work, I feel a deep quiet and solitude and perhaps loneliness. If I didn't describe the tension between being alone and being lonely, I don't think I could actually convey what I was seeing when I stood before it at the Whitney. His works, so blank, are almost workbooks waiting to be filled. Think Keats' Negative Capability or scriptural Midrash.

While I don't consider ekphrasis and translation to be synonymous terms or activities, both pose an intensely difficult question. "Is this my own personal association and reaction, bound only to my own experience, or is this a universally accessible way to turn this image into words?" I'm thankful I don't have to be the judge. I've got buddies that could crush this far better than me but, imperfect as it is, it just feels so sumptuous to try. Looking and describing felt really good.

BINA

A Book Is a River

a book is a river;
  a voyage into the unknown
    on a paper boat.
      a book is a harbour
        where boats meet,
          bearing parables and thoughts;
          a book is a searchlight
          illuminating thoughts
        rooted in a forest;
      a book is a forest,
        its leaves dense with words
          its words are flames kindling our senses;
          a book is the sum of all our senses
          that flow like a river;
            a book is a river of words
            that encircles
              the universe;
            a book
         is the universe of life;
      life that unskeins
      a constellation of experiences
      ways of living and seeing
        and telling;
          a book is a river;
          a book is forever.

Commentary

Just as the crow flies at will onto my windowsill ... so do stray thoughts arrive at random to perch on the windows of my mind ... waiting to be fed with words that will fly into the open skies of imagination.

It was in the late fifties when the stillness of a classroom of 10-year-old students diligently writing their exam papers got me musing. Having completed my papers early, I would turn my dreary question paper around to liven it with my vagabond scribbles. Little poems would emerge along with drawings ... whimsical forays into a playful world of make-belief.

Reading became a compulsion through the years, novels and poetry, books on art and gradually, philosophy and politics. Words were a constant companion ... always around to nudge me into a universe of rumination. In step with words was an irresistible seduction of the fine arts. Words and images thus often conjugated to emerge as ekphrastic poems; and the luminosity of unvarnished, raw thoughts found resonance in my writings.

Also, having lived in Japan in my mid-twenties, another world was gifted to me. The essentials of aesthetics, minimalism, and a joyful rigor for perfection. Perhaps because of these critical learnings, my writings veered towards the compactness of thoughts ... haiku, tanka and the magic of haibun ... all of which became my footsteps through poems that were largely small. The long ones happened too ... occasionally, but they were always marginalized by the little ones!

Veering towards an expression naked in its simplicity, became my vocabulary. While my poems through most of my life were hidden in a closet of doubt, the need to share thoughts in recent years, was perhaps a 'coming out' from my introverted space ... to inhabit a convening of minds. Since then, six books of poetry and one of haiku emerged joyously ... with many poems translated into Mandarin, Spanish, French, Greek, Arabic and Urdu.

Words can be messengers. Life can be beautiful....

Simon Collings

A perfectly still day

The woman in a pink sweatshirt was drifting across the park, several feet above the ground. 'Help,' she shouted. 'For Christ's sake, someone help.' Jason jumped and managed to catch hold of one of her legs as she floated by. He was almost lifted off his feet, as though caught by a strong current, but he held on. With the help of a passing dog walker he managed to steer the woman to a bench, where they tethered her by an ankle to the back of the seat using the dog's lead. The woman floated there like a party balloon. 'I'm going to be sick,' she announced, and promptly vomited. Seconds later they noticed two more figures drifting overhead, too high to be reached. One was a young man in hi-viz overalls and a hard hat who was holding a length of plastic tubing. The other, also male, wore a dark blue suit and tan shoes. The man in overalls tried to catch hold of a tree branch as he passed but couldn't reach. They were moving at a steady pace even though the day was perfectly still.

Commentary

I was introduced to the work of U.S. artist Alex Prager by my partner, who thought I would find her work interesting. The first images I saw were stills and clips from her short film *Run*, which in surreal Technicolor portrays the stress of living through uncertain times. Searching for more examples, I came across the extraordinary sequence of photographs called *The Mountain*, images of ordinary everyday people floating above the ground against a clear sky. They have a quality which is both magical and unnerving. The images prompted an immediate picture in my mind of a woman in distress drifting over a park and man trying to catch her. The poem grew from this.

At the time, my partner and I were supporting two Ukrainian families who had come to the UK as refugees. Their sense of uprootedness, disorientation, and uncertainty about the future was a constant presence, and our attempts to try to help them felt like trying to grab hold of someone drifting past on the wind. Our friends were educated, professional, smartly dressed, much like the people in Prager's images. This connection is perhaps why Prager's photographs took on that feeling of dislocation, stress and anxiety we were experiencing with our Ukrainian friends.

I had read very little about *The Mountain* before viewing the images. I learned later that the photographs were, in fact, a response to Covid lockdowns and for Prager they were expressive of a sense of ecstatic release and freedom on emerging from the pandemic. But by this time the poem had taken on a life of its own, closer to the atmosphere of *Run*. It was about a different kind of weightlessness, almost the flipside of what *The Mountain* addresses. *Run* is in fact 'part 2' to the 'part 1' which is *The Mountain*.

My text, as is usually the case when I'm responding to a stimulus from another artwork, doesn't seek to represent the original but to record my reaction, however personal and subjective that might be. It's more a response to Prager's work generally than to a specific photograph. I love the ambiguity, hyperreal and filmic, in her pictures. I aim to produce something of that same mysteriousness and unease in the images I create textually.

The poem was a visceral response to Prager's images, not an intellectual one. I was describing a scene in my mind provoked by the photographs. I did not have any message to convey, and the interpretations I offer above only occurred to me later. Writing the poem is a process of trying to discover more of the image, of listening for the words that come if you're patient, revealing more of the scene, the woman vomiting, the other people passing out of reach. The piece emerged over a period of a few days.

Hedy Habra

Or How Can We Ever Cut Down to the Bare Essentials?

after Vagabond *by Remedios Varo*

He kept retreating from room to room, feeling the weight of all the furniture and mementos staring at him like deceased relatives. It was as though the house wrapped layers of time around him, confining him inside a pod about to burst open. For a while he'd only use his bedroom and the kitchen. He eventually retreated to the sunroom. Its walls lined with bookshelves comforted him as he lay on the wicker couch opposite the bay window. He soon realized he needed fewer meals and only one change of clothes.

His lightness became manifest when feathers seemed to grow out of his bones, filling him with a desire to embrace the movements of the wind. He tried to get rid of plants, of his archived papers, of the photos that couldn't find their place in the abandoned albums and the books he knew he'd never read or reread. Finally, the day came when unable to break all ties, he clung to his tabby, the photo of a woman, a purple-lipped cattleya, a few books, anything he could hide under his strong wings, slammed the door and left.

Commentary

I have a passion for visual art, and I'm also an artist. As I was growing up, my mother's artwork covered the walls of our home. I used to engage in a dialogue with the characters in her paintings and daydreamed of entering their world. My passion for writing the image is an extension of such exposure. When I write ekphrastic poetry, I do not aim at offering a mere description of the work of art but rather attempt to express my response to it. I sometimes address the artist and try to imagine his or her creative process and delve under the brushstrokes to unravel hidden meanings or create a new version of the artwork, using the music and colors of language as tools. I usually use the image as a point of departure for an oneiric or surreal recreation departing from the original. It is at times an attempt at transforming a two-dimensional representation into a three-dimensional, almost cinematic rendition that involves all five senses. I also aim at offering an imagined version of what might have happened before or after the portrayed scene, oftentimes from the point of view of one of the characters in the paintings.

Most of my poems are persona poems, but I find myself impelled to project my inner world onto the world of the painting as though I were inhabiting the visual art, which triggers repressed or unconscious emotions. When I set up to write about a painting, I take a picture of the artwork and place it where I can look at it daily. The space of the canvas turns into a sort of mandala that leads to meditation, and numerous drafts. I feel that the shape of an ekphrastic prose poem evokes a framed tapestry or an artwork presented visually on the page. As a result, the original will never be viewed in the same way and will retain traces of the verbal images. Every artwork seems to determine the way a poem will be written. When my search for the arresting detail in a composition eludes me, I resort to the constraints of a form like a pantoum, whose repetitions help me narrow down keywords and images.

Over the years, I have been inspired by a variety of artists of different styles and periods, but I have a predilection for the surreal because it explores the dream psyche. One of my favorite artists is the Spanish-born Mexican Remedios Varo (1908–1963), whose work inspired a great number of my poems. I find many layers of interpretation in her oneiric art imbued with archetypal patterns. I wrote "Or How Can We Ever Cut Down To The Bare Essentials?" after Varo's *Vagabond*. In this prose poem, I imagined a character gradually desisting from what had represented his life quest, ending up holding onto what meant the most to him. I saw it as a freeing attempt at shaking habits and societal impositions. I felt deeply in my own life this necessary movement towards eliminating the surplus accumulated over the years, realizing how what was once meaningful becomes irrelevant with time, not only to our children but also to us. This poem also reflects my feelings during the pandemic when so many of our priorities shifted and a lot that was valued ceased to matter. Although rooted in reality, the poem opens a door to the surreal on account of my love for fabulist authors and Latin American magical realism.

Ruth Stacey

View from Drahim Castle

Boots clang out the bell in the heart of the wooden planks; the
bridge is built out of boats moored together. Once upon a tune.
The water whips the air into this hush and rush of shrillness.
The cold should freshen the face, but it settles like fog, prising
and chilling the skin, or slaps it – the shock of this mirrored
the pathway through the swampland. The crest of each hillock,
every emergence from the woods, there was a beast. The teeth.
The claws. The shudder is yellow. Now, ahead, a new part of
the parchment is unfolded. Clouds retreat, the deciduous trees
have air around them, the oak tree stretches into a cloak. Green
is mint, geranium, peapods. My horse flexes its tendons into
a gallop, past deer grazing the soft-spun grasses. There is a
ruined castle. I must explore it. My curiosity is lavender-tinted,
rose-scented, a flower which unfolds each petal to reveal a
question mark – a golden key. The curve is silver, the ball is a
copper pearl. At the top of the castle, richer than the treasure
I gather, a balcony and view. I stand there. It is I who beholds
this, though I is another. The sky has never seemed so wide
in this world. The sun warms a walled city that ribbons the
landscape. Terracotta roof tiles wrap each tower. Most timber
framed buildings are sheltered by the grey stone walls, yet some
gather outside like hopeful dogs. The city paints itself into a
triangle; the eye is drawn to the high tower. Flames beckon.
Myself is eager to leave, shifts weight so our metal clinks. I
hold myself steady to stare some more – pages of fantasy books
paper the interior of a heart.

Commentary

The Witcher 3: Wild Hunt is an action role-playing game with a third-person perspective, that takes the player on a journey through different landscapes. The player becomes a monster hunter traversing this dangerous world. For this ekphrastic poem I replayed an area of the game for the ambience and to renew my memory, and then used a still image from the game to describe. The first main playable area is called Velen, a war-torn swampland. It is oppressive, with brutal imagery and storm filled skies, so that when the player leaves the area and enters the land approaching the free city of Novigrad, tension dissipates and the area is more tranquil and verdant. I chose this scene as I found it very emotive when I saw it in the game. The poem has a symbolist approach, meaning that I purposely aimed for an enigmatic and dreamy style, utilizing fragments to layer meaning and point of view so nothing is certain, and the reader must actively puzzle out what the subject matter is referring to. There are references to fairy tale to root the reader in this fantastical setting, as well as the description of the city in the scene, which aims to evoke it like a painting for the reader. I wanted the poem to be rich with sensory detail and used half rhyme to create a musical effect throughout. The heart of the poem is a playful use of Rimbaud's statement *Je est un autre* ('I is another'), to represent the layered effect of player and character, the many selves present in the poem and game. The ungrammatical moment 'myself is eager to leave' is deliberately jarring, like Rimbaud's statement, reminding the reader the self is not singular, rather it is layered. The poem ends by focusing on this scene of the city prompting the memory in the player of previously read fantasy books, yet this thought is outside the immersion of roleplaying as the character and the needs of the quest in the game. For a moment, the layered self is aware of this doubling, and I wanted to use the metaphor of playing the game, and this awareness or sense of the collage of selves, to represent Rimbaud's statement about sense of poetic self being separate or other from the persona, witnessing as a thought is conjured and becomes something enigmatic on the page.

KANE HOLBORN

Self Portrait of Someone Else's Self Portrait

after Painting *by Tayler Holborn, 2020*

I dislocate my face.
I have Cubist genetics,
built of blue neurology:
humanism made disposable.
Remake the artifice
again. Coloured myself,
blue-faced, back together.
Daubed-over layers of
unfashionable brown.
Memories forgotten, painted,
remembered.
Cybernetic blue jigsawed
by a painter
with Surrealist furniture
forming a portrait détourned,
a rusty aquatic thing
whose bones shaped memory
jagged-red.
A blue neurological thing
looking at me,
left-hemisphere eyes
redirected.
Shoulders mountain-made.
Barb-wired teeth

introverted into listening instruments
jolting the eyes awake.

Commentary

Using the Tool of (In)verse Ekphrasis

Writing poetry is filtered through a particular tool I call '(in) verse ekphrasis'. (In)verse ekphrasis allows me to discuss issues of representation adjacent to my own (dis)ability. There is always a sense of parallax in any idea of ekphrasis. Simply describing this as a parallax view from a 'disabled poet' would mean misrepresenting myself as a poet. The term 'disabled poet' casts limitations upon my creative practice because it renders me less than I am. I am a poet who is disabled, that is true. And my physical and internal view of the world is to some extent governed by this factor. But as a descriptor it undermines the word poet. When a non-disabled poet is described as an able poet, it comes as a form of compliment. The word 'disabled' itself is problematic. Terms other poets used to describe their differences with words like 'disabled' and 'crippled' stand out as particularly harmful to a contemporary, progressive understanding of (dis)ability. My poem 'Self-Portrait of Someone Else's Self-Portrait' demonstrates (in)verse ekphrasis as a way of critically responding to visual representations of (dis)ability.

I used the ekphrastic process when I was inspired by a painting by the artist and my brother Tayler Holborn. In terms of my ekphrastic process, therefore, I drew inspiration while watching as the canvas was painted. My creative and critical thinking in this instance has to do with drafts, for as my brother experimented with color and shape I wrote as the painting took form. My process was as much a creative intervention on the painting, as well as an intervention on ekphrasis itself, in writing imagistically about aspects of my life responding to disability.

I am using this poem in order to explore the new way I am using ekphrasis to highlight the perceived image of my disability. While I wasn't the inspiration for my brother's painting, by repainting myself through the tool of (in)verse ekphrasis, I am drawing on his creative process as a way of examining myself in a pictorial sense, and this relates to how I am being ekphrastic in describing my experiences of disability through visual poetic terms. Through what I can only describe as a different kind of 'reverse ekphrasis' (I call this tool '[in]verse ekphrasis') I am making myself and my disability visible through my poems by highlighting my own unseen narrative of disability within the interplay of my poems visually.

Considering my intervention with ekphrasis, Marcelle Freiman (2020:1) leads me in her essay 'Unstated and Vital,' in which she describes how ekphrastic poems would not emerge without 'an external object, image or artwork. Although a draft can be produced in the space of "seeing" and writing, there are many implicit and unstated associations and processes (half-registered, or not conscious at all, but still there) in the space between the engagement with artwork or object and the act of writing.'

Using ekphrasis as a tool, therefore, is my way of seeing art and producing poetry, because I am adapting the idea and writing using disability images. For example, the experiences and situations I am presenting skew and queer those discussed even by published disabled poets. Images as obscure as toilets prompt my readers into new ways of seeing situations related to my disability previously unseen and not widely considered in mainstream terms. Through working with ekphrasis in my poetry, I explore contemporary reactions to the perceived images of my disability, relating to how I am using the concept to write about the unseen space of disablement.

Works cited:

Freiman, M. (2020) Unstated and Vital. Ekphrasis, cognition, and a briefcase, *Axon Journal* 10:1. Available at: https://www.axonjournal.com.au/issue-vol-10-no-1-may-2020/unstated-and-vital [Accessed 14 July 2020].

Holborn, T . (2020), *Painting*. Available at: https://theanystage.wixsite.com/kaneholborn/collaborations

Bob Beagrie

The Painted Peasantry

after Johannes Vermeer

You'd never guess what this year has cost
in a shepherd's flock of counted sheep
passing behind closed eyelids in the dark –
the yan, tan, tether of each soft fleece,
as the rest of the household shift in sleep
rinsing yesterday's smudges and stains
without removing its grease, or else plaiting
the wickerwork sallows of bread baskets
through stints of rapid eye movement;
and as if by magic the chore's complete

with a practiced, thankful ease, see how
she pours fresh milk from a terracotta jug
into the waiting bowl as the morning pours
lightness with a flourish into the scullery
and fills it to the brim with clarity, colour,
worldly edges, surfaces, class distinctions:
the quiet tiles, the plaster-smooth cheek,
plain linen headscarf, a dimple on the chin
familial and homely as the baker's pattern
on scored dough, risen to a crusted loaf

as comely as the tune of enduring milk-fall,
notes of pearly bubbles, surface bevels
suggest some undertow compensating

for the steady flow of a brush's strokes,
the kindly, calculating, ever-captivated gaze
although she seems content upon his canvas
composed to the confines of maidenhood
she learned early to conceal the stirrings
buttoned with prayer beneath a bodice,
buried somewhere deep in pinafore folds

who knows what future swills in the bowl,
or whether her tilted ear catches desire
like the shower of a skylark's song-flight
blessing bulbs in the beds of a tulip field?

Commentary

'The Painted Peasantry' is based on Johannes Vermeer's *The Milkmaid*, sometimes called *The Kitchen Maid*, painted in 1657–1658. As ekphrasis aims to illuminate meanings within an original artwork through written description, the poem attempts to highlight details within the painting, objects and their arrangements, features of the setting, surfaces, textures, the tones of the milkmaid's skin and headscarf. There is a formality to the composition which the poem emulates in its arrangement of three ten-line stanzas with a four-line coda and heightened language.

What strikes me is the study of light, the contrasts of shade and luminosity, how they form, on a two-dimensional canvas, a viscosity of space around the subject. The poem pays homage to this artistry, 'as the morning pours lightness with a flourish into the scullery / and fills it to the brim with clarity'. Vermeer's subjects are isolated by the light and darkness between them, like the figures inhabiting separate bubbles of living within Edward Hopper's paintings. The fact I wrote this poem during a Covid-19 lockdown may have given this interpretation added emotional significance.

What can a poem bring to a painting, what can ekphrasis offer beyond description and homage to painterly skill? The poem begins with the casual address to the reader's/viewer's lack of understanding of the struggles that lie beneath or beyond the temporal frame of the painting. The milkmaid's labor, the labor of shepherds, spinners seamstresses, basket maker, baker etc, and behind the verisimilitude itself. There is an implied sacrifice of labor as 'the rest of the household shift in sleep' while the work is done. Like all manual labor, the expertise and grace come from long hours of repetition until "as if by magic the chore's complete."

A poem can animate the uncanny stillness of an image; the suspended flow of milk into the bowl resumes with 'pearly bubbles, surface bevels,' which introduces the painter's flow of brushstrokes, and his gaze. The power relations between subject and viewer come into play, the decorum of the classical pose represents learned labor of social station, restraint, etiquette. There are repressions involved in this, by both subject and painter, status transactions in the act of observing and being observed. The coda hints at scrying, notes unconscious desires, and widens the lens to the Dutch landscape, marked by the dynamic between industrialized tulip fields and the wild jouissance of a skylark's song.

Holly Iglesias

Cathedral Window, Cologne

My concern is never art, but always what art can be used for.
—Gerhart Richter

Tracery of light framed in the stone and mortar of faith, all of it wrought by history and a vision determined to defy meaning, to show nothing but the thing itself—eleven thousand squares of hand-blown glass, seventy-two colors in a random pattern. Stripped of symbol and cipher, the window thwarts the brain, deranges the senses into silence, forcing the eyes to come to rest as everything else is carried off, like the dust to which we all return, like the dust of the rubble that once was Cologne, May, 1942, the cathedral, seven centuries old, shattered as the Allied bombings began, making infernos of ancient cities, Mainz, Hamburg, Stuttgart, Bremen, Münster, Kiel, Augsburg, Dresden. Dresden, where Richter was born, Richter who wanted the window to have something self-evident like the play of light altering the colors, changing where they fall as the day progresses, as they float across the floor of the transept, that place where horizontal and vertical meet.

Commentary

I may have come late to poetry, but that arrival quickly took me to prose poems and to ekphrasis. My first protracted writing project eventually became my first book, *Souvenirs of a Shrunken World,* based on the Louisiana Purchase Exposition, the world's fair held in St. Louis in 1904, the largest such fair ever held. Because many people by that time could afford a Kodak camera, there exists an extensive archive of photographs taken of this colossal event by amateur as well as professional photographers. The structures at the fair, despite their grandeur, were built to be demolished easily once the event concluded, thus creating instant nostalgia in the hearts of the nearly 20 million people who attended during the nine months the fair was open. Because there would be no trace left behind, snapshots and picture postcards became treasures, small remnants to remind the visitor of the transitory paradise where she had whiled away a day, or two, or three.

This experience led me to study documentary photography in general and I continued to use photos as poetry prompts, especially from the trove of work commissioned by the U.S. Farm Security Administration during the Depression to enlist empathy for the poor and dispossessed. But in 2002, my sense of what art could do was thoroughly transformed when I saw Gerhard Richter's picture-paintings on display at the Museum of Modern Art in New York. On first glance, the images—of SS officers, including one of the artist's uncle, and of members of the Baader-Meinhof guerrilla group—appeared to be faded newspaper clippings or old snapshots. But as the viewer drew closer, the clearer it became that these were in fact oil paintings made to evoke the look of such things long stored in a dark and dusty corner. Richter's use of a visual medium to question modes of perception, of art's relation to history, of the reliability of public memory, made an indelible impression on me.

I had begun to realize how much of my work were series of prose poems that conveyed sweeps of history through small objects or from the point of view of bystanders in shock—the big story told through the little story, the dulled yet urgent voice of trauma. I became obsessed with the rubble, detritus, the heaps of ash under which the evidence of the past is buried. (Think of Walter Benjamin's description of Klee's *Angel of History*.) When I learned that Richter had been commissioned to create a new stained-glass window for the medieval cathedral of Cologne, I felt compelled to learn about his process of creation and how his mind grappled with the place where destruction and revival intersected. "Cathedral Window, Cologne" grew out of this meditation on Richter's act of restoration.

Oz Hardwick

Electronic no. 1

Light circles and Earth calls,
an almost-**language** of chalkscreech,
reflected metal of an open iris, closing.

Coordinates shift. See-saw surge
of falling up to a floating/crushing
interface with earth. Ripple and freeze.

Blue Marble revolves. Far below,
shadows clip neat coasts, a criss-cross map
of crabs and lions scoured in sand.

Ghost cities bleed radiation, and I
wave, **weightless**, roped to the void,
chasing myself in repeating circles.

Traces tack patterns **across** a tiled floor
in an airless can, where Iris echoes
refract, recede, reflect insubstantial depths.

I hear drift   sigh   negative   space
whispers   and I   step   out
on   a   planet   with   no   surface   but

fantastic
planet
final
programme
space
ritual
count
brass
sleeper
journey
tomorrow
people
brainbox
pollution
angel's
egg
breathe
today
we
choose
faces
cyborg
f(r)iction.

Commentary

It is 1973. A friend and I are sitting in my family's bathroom, he on the laundry box and I on the toilet seat. I'm 13, he's 12, and we're here because the tiled space makes the ropey mono cassette player sound better than it does anywhere else in the house. It's plugged into the shaver socket, and we are listening to Hawkwind's *Space Ritual* for the first time.

1973: possibly the last hurrah for the future. On 19th December 1972, Apollo 17 – the last manned mission to the Moon as I type this – had returned with the iconic "Blue Marble" photograph of the Earth, the one that shows the whole disc of the planet brightly illuminated for the first and so-far final time. Closer to home, British underground stalwarts Hawkwind, on the back of their surprise hit single 'Silver Machine', had been trucking their all-singing, all-dancing, lysergic space-fest around packed halls. They'd been playing in Swansea as the last men on the Moon splashed down, and tapes from Liverpool on the 22nd and London on the 30th had been edited and overdubbed into the sprawling *Space Ritual*. The lavishly-packaged double album was released on 11th May 1973, three days before Skylab was launched, with all its problems, system failures, and subsequent repairs when the crew arrived later in the month, heralding in a new era of space investigation which, though we couldn't know it at the time, would be a hell of a lot less interesting for schoolboys.

I could write a book about the impact discovering Hawkwind had on me, and this was the first of their albums I listened to in stunned silence from start to finish. It contains a couple of tracks which have subsequently become rock classics, some of the best examples of their distinctive penchant for implacable, mantra-like repetition and, most significantly for me, passages of spoken word which drift and flash amongst electronic sounds which conjure impossible dimensions of imagined space. The brief interlude titled 'Electronic no. 1,' though, has no words. It's 2½ minutes of pure space, reminiscent of Bebe and Louis Barron, and of the BBC Radiophonic Workshop, but here foregrounded, rather than soundtracking Daleks or Robby the Robot.

I'd discover Pierre Schaeffer, Karlheinz Stockhausen, et al, in time, but what swam in to populate and illuminate the vast depths between sounds on that first listen, was the dazzling galaxy of books, comics, TV, film, posters, and music which orbited the scientific moment of 1973. The effect on me was so profound that, every time I have heard it subsequently, a part of me has been in that small, tiled bathroom, somewhere on that shining blue marble, with a crew of astronauts invisibly smiling down from around 270 miles above. Part of each listening experience is the repeated iteration of that originary epiphanic encounter, shocking in its immediacy, while simultaneously conjoined with a profound awareness of the widening distance between the present moment and that first occasion; between who I am now and that new teenager still full of wonder for imagined futures. It's like the end of Ray Bradbury's oft-anthologized 1949 story 'Kaleidoscope', which I must have first read about then, and which would influence the end of John Carpenter's 1974 'Waiting for Godot in outer space' movie, *Dark Star*. I am those astronauts drifting apart, becoming distracted by the huge beauty and inevitability of it all, leaving bright traces of words ...

... and ...

... and here I am drawn into the ever-expanding hauntological apprehension of a future that never was, 'Stone

Tape Theory', and Charles Babbage's still-resounding voice as he suggests that 'The air itself is one vast library on whose pages are for ever written all that man has ever said or woman whispered. There, in their mutable but unerring characters, mixed with the earliest, as well as with the latest sighs of mortality, stand for ever recorded, vows unredeemed, promises unfulfilled, perpetuating in the united movements of each particle, the testimony of man's changeful will' (*The Ninth Bridgewater Treatise* [1937]). Only here—wherever "here" is— I'm in a vacuum beyond air and there is only the language of void and imagination, glittering fragments which speak of the things for which I don't have neat words, but have been trying to articulate since 1973.

The Electric Score:

Babbage, Charles. *The Ninth Bridgewater Treatise*, 2nd ed. (London: John Murray, 1838).

Bradbury, Ray. "Kaleidoscope," in *Short Stories Volume 1* (London: Harper Voyager, 2008): 155-62.

Coverley, Merlin. *Hauntology* (Harpenden: Oldcastle, 2020).

Hawkwind, "Electronic no. 1" (Del Dettmar/Dik Mik), from *The Space Ritual Alive in Liverpool and London* (United Artists, 1973).

Pearson, Neil (ed.). *Apollo VII–XVII* (Kempen: teNeuss, 2018).

JANE BURN

The Abstract and the Anonymous: Poetic Translations of Victor Pasmore's *The Green Earth, 1979–80, Apollo Pavilion, 1969, & Transformation 7, 1970–1971*

an idea of Earth   a good green Earth
where colour makes us islands   where everything is lichen
                            eukaryotic bloom feeding on light
                            a devotion of moss
            elliptic lakes
see how poems bloom with curious forms
                the cadence of leaves fallen upon a pond
tree crowns seen from the sky   kelp and wrack
nothing is air   written into each inlet
            around each atoll
an idea of Earth
an ecstasy of nothing   a good green
                an Earth breathing
a future built from geometry
no gilded icon for this artificial place
a community remade on abstract planes
            this is a brutal heritage
            and it belongs exactly here

was meant, Pasmore said, [to be] *a free*
and anonymous monument   a synthesis
of dream and shape   idea and interaction
                          a poetry of henge
                          and block
      a concrete lyric
      a graphic villanelle
      a vision of real-life existence
      a catacomb for biomorphic ghosts
scrawled on, played in, fought in, fucked against
waste your human warmth against its grout skin
                 it is used to your
                   misunderstanding
it does not care if you see it or if you don't

        here on the page
      all I know is written into
     shapes   the thing I feel
   the most is   Blue and Blue says
can you teach the   sky? I see how
   the sun, how   the heat of the day
  is all about the   passing through
  of white light   and the diffusing
  of Blue light   scattering on
molecules of air   and the way
  I am designed is   to see Blue
    best of all   it is all
    about the   length
     of waves

> Blue is the taste
> of the sea   the body
> of water offers   it back
> to my eyes   Blue says
> can you sing   the way
> I hold on to   your
> heart?

Note:

The Apollo Pavilion, a divisive piece of public art was designed by Victor Pasmore and built in 1969 in Peterlee, County Durham. Peterlee was founded under the New Towns Act of 1946, mainly housing coal miners and their families who had been moved from historical pit village communities.

a free and anonymous monument Farmer, Graham & Pendlebury, John.

Commentary

Victor Pasmore (1908–1988) spent his artistic life in experimentations of form, medium and genre. He produced works in print, architecture, sculpture and paintings, mapping both the figurative and the abstract. What I sense most strongly in Pasmore's output is an eternal, thrilling and explorative dialogue between positive and negative shapes, between occupied and unoccupied space. For him, art's dialectic was an '... [attempt] to see ... how the complexities of a fully realized image might emerge from, or be broken down into, highly abstract formal structures of shape and rhythm and colour.' (Purdon, 2017)

I return time and time again to Pasmore's shapeshifting body of work. Within it I encounter a mirror to inspire and validate my own polymathic, hybrid approach to the creative process, my own passionate study of white space upon the page. I wanted my poem to articulate these negotiations between that which shall or shall not be represented, together with alternations between geometric or organic form and the unspoken inhabitancy of liminal space. The words alive yet invisible within. Pasmore may have '... reduced his visual language to include only the simplest of shapes and patterns ...' (Barcio, 2017) but it remains an incredibly powerful language nevertheless.

I contemplate the beautiful paradoxes arising from his work. Take, for example, the Apollo Pavilion: which is deemed to be most important – its concrete scaffold, or the sky, framed around and within its presence? One cannot be experienced without the other. One cannot take precedence over the other. One informs and nourishes the other. The same goes for human residence (and I mean 'residence' to include physical experience of the building, or experience through drawings, photographs, or accessible descriptions). Does architecture only exist because we place our presence within it? How do its lines, corners and windows attract or repel us? Against its harsh walls, do we become just another of Pasmore's biomorphic silhouettes? Are we absorbed by the art we experience? Is this necessarily a bad thing?

One cannot balance such marvelous quandaries without the existence of both objective and subjective thinking. My poem travels toward and away from this Pasmore inheritance – ekphrasis for me goes well beyond description of the artwork itself. The third-party observer adds their own layers of interpretation, becoming another link in the ekphrasis chain. Art as idea translates to art in existence, to person bearing witness, to poetic form. Readers of the said poem stretch the chain yet further, as no two individuals' reactions to the poem will be the same, and should anyone write an ekphrastic response to my poem, then the chain becomes interesting indeed.

I have carried forward his heritage of dualism and allowed for the addition of my emotionally resonating self by including the imagery his artworks brought into being in my mind, rather than what he may have specifically meant them to mean. Pasmore worked '… not in a purely naturalistic way but not in an entirely abstract way either …' (Barcio, 2017), and in this I sense the permission to 'read' a 'devotion of moss' or 'an ecstasy of nothing' into his suggestive abstract semblances, as well as permission to leap away from standard, regulated lines.

Yes, I have set my own strictures, but these textual portions are satellites – each able to function alone, each a written manifestation of an ekphrasis chain. The interplay between text and blank has further served to embody the abstract. The poem's layout suggests both the building's plan and his abstract artwork – the milder curves and the harsher straights. When the poem is asked to progress its translation further, it becomes a different creature again – a creature of variable solidity, a broken puzzle happy to remain unfixed.

I have attempted to write in flux, allowing for the subtlety and sharpness of space. I have echoed his use of the lyrical and the abstract, or, as Pasmore himself preferred to describe it, 'independent painting' (*Victor Pasmore: The Final Decades*, 2023). My poem is a reflection of the curious conflict between so many of his curvilinear, gorgeously colored abstract paintings and prints and the harsh, linear Apollo Pavilion and surrounding Sunny Blunts Estate, also designed by Pasmore (located in Peterlee, County Durham). This quote from Pasmore, featured in the Marlborough Fine Art exhibition catalog, *The Image in Search of Itself. New Paintings 1969–71*, was held at the heart of my engagement with this particular ekphrasis work:

Today meaning dissolves in order to create new meaning and what is known becomes unknown. In art the peripheral images of thought and perception reappear as anonymous objects before which is always a question. While reason sleeps the symbol awakes.

Works Cited and Consulted:

Barcio, Phillip. How Victor Pasmore Found His True Style in Abstraction. *IdeelArt*, 14th August, 2014. https://www.ideelart.com/magazine/victor-pasmore

Farmer, Graham & Pendlebury, John. Conserving Dirty Concrete: The Decline and Rise of Pasmore's Apollo Pavilion, Peterlee. *Journal of Urban Design* Volume 18, May 2013.

ResearchGate.   https://www.researchgate.net/figure/Axonometric-of-Apollo-Pavilion-Source-Drawing-by-Graham-Farmer_fig2_263555356

Purdon, James. The shifting styles of Victor Pasmore. *Apollo Magazine*, 2017. https://www.apollo-magazine.com/the-shifting-styles-of-victor-pasmore/

Victor Pasmore: The Final Decades, Marlborough, 2023. https://www.marlboroughnewyork.com/exhibitions/victor-pasmore-the-final-decades#tab:slideshow;tab-1:slideshow;slide:5

DeWitt Henry

Andrew Wyeth

Walking north, while traffic passed,
I saw from Bridge Street bridge
upstream, where the current hits rocks
and broken concrete from blocks
that once held waterwheels for the
brick-walled mills on opposite banks,
how midday sun struck a lower casement
on the far building, which reflected its image,
distinct as a photograph, bright on
the dark spill, foam and rush,
where the current swirled back,
a counter wave, and the main
flow kept straight and under the bridge.
All that drama! Commotion!
Vivid yellows, reds, browns, brick,
reeds, grasses (a quiet pool below
to my left, where two geese paddled),
turquoise sky, green, swift and constant
flow, the image of the window
projected, complete with silhouette
of a tree branch, like a carpet,
floating, fixed. I paused to let
these marvels register; then kept on
in my crossing, heading home.
Even time of day was part,
fall into winter. Eterne in mutability.

One more canvas Andrew Wyeth failed
to capture, paint, and frame.

Commentary

My first close-up experience of an Andrew Wyeth painting was *Wind From the Sea*, which hung on loan in my college's art museum when I was a freshman. An open, weathered window frame (probably from inside Christina Olson's house in Maine), with ragged, tattered curtains lifted by a breeze. "Ordinary," commentators point out; yet rich with drama and meticulous caring and invention on the artist's part, all that detail! Curtain fibers, like ... well, hair. Or wild sea grass. And haunted by the painter's emotions, and by the invisible forces of nature. A breath of spring on the worn and transitory.

In following decades, I absorbed what I then assumed to be the Wyeth oeuvre. A hundred or so paintings reproduced in *LIFE* magazine, then collected in books, following on curated exhibitions, etc. Publication of his long-hidden series, *The Helga pictures*, caused a stir in 1987. Wyeth died in 2009, but it was not until after his wife and executor Betsy's death in 2020 that as many as 10,000 images (paintings, sketches, and notebook studies) became public.

Since then, I've followed a Facebook page dedicated to Wyeth, and its seemingly inexhaustible feed of unfamiliar Wyeths. I've come to realize how mannered his subjects and compositions could be, so at times he seems to be imitating himself. But also how he kept working at given subjects, version after version, until inspiration kicked in.

He spiritualized a lived domestic and local world, with objects, perspectives, and props of daily use. He loved eternal forces, of light, of wind, of heat and cold, of time itself, and how they met and shaped resistances. In *Monday Morning*, what is the drama of an oval wicker wash-basket left out and leaned lengthwise against an outside wall? Remnants of snow remain in its bottom curve. Its season of human use is just returning, announced by morning sunlight striking it slant, and casting its striated and elongated shadow across the ground and up the improbable angles of a triangle-shaped basement bulkhead. Sun meets wicker and casts a shadow seemingly beyond prediction, and which even suggests menace as it ends in a sharp point. Wyeth and Robert Frost were mutual admirers, I've read, sharing a sense of commonplace shocks and recognitions.

Ekphrastic poetry usually pays "inter-media" respect to visual art, from Achilles' shield in Homer to the Grecian urn in Keats' "Ode." My poem, however, seeks to evoke an experience that Wyeth for all his oeuvre never noticed or imagined, yet which is reinforced, if not inspired by his example.

The phenomenon my poem describes is one I've never before noticed in nature or in art: a reflection, caused by fall sunlight, off a window near running water and cast as a glowing replica, like a fixed and floating carpet, on a constant wave of fast-spilling current: a natural marvel of choreography, the mystery of which is contradiction.

Rupert M. Loydell

Barjac

*A palette cannot become a bird just because it
is adorned with wings with discernible feathers.*
—Danièle Cohn, *Anselm Kiefer Studios*

Built unthinkable towers on stage,
in glass boxes and then outside,
used meat hooks to hang stones,
cracked clay, melted mud and metal,
strung warships up in glasshouse
skies, crash landed aeroplanes
on puddled industrial floors.

A torn child's smock hangs
amid burnt detritus, faded
paint, dirt and dust. Plants
invade the rafters, the trees
have turned to rust. My books
are too heavy to read or own.

I abandoned my own museum,
moved away from the ruins to
some place else. Sculptures
teeter in haphazard piles,
walls reinforce themselves.

Climb the stairs. You may
be able to learn to fly with

painted wings. Or decide to
fail in other people's rooms.

I do not hope to lift the veil,
am happy to confuse; everyone
must explain it for themselves.

Time is reversed, off-kilter,
always out of balance.

It is impossible to paint with ice.

Commentary

Able to Fly

The end of second semester and the undergraduate year at the university where I work is when books make their way back to the library shelves. It is when I make sure to visit and borrow the latest catalogues and critical volumes, along with anything else that catches my eye.

As a poet and artist, I am fascinated by the processes used to write and paint, along with sketchbooks and studios (somehow, writing desks don't have the same allure!), and this year my borrowed books included a couple about Anselm Keifer's studio/exhibition complex in Barjac in the South of France which, as the website explains, the artist 'has transformed [...] into a uniquely immersive artistic environment, creating numerous installations, often at monumental scale'.

Kiefer's work often appears huge, especially when contained in traditional gallery spaces, but La Ribaute, constructed and developed over 30 years, is home to sculptures, environments and installations which could not possibly be shown in the white boxes where we usually view contemporary art.

I've never been a fan of Kiefer's work, often finding it polemical and clumsily made, sometimes over-reliant on size to dwarf viewers and overpower any criticism they might have. However, one exhibition I saw in London in 1989 did intrigue: massive lead books, an unreadable library of metal. Other works can seem almost kitsch as they (according to the Gagosian website) 'reflect upon Germany's post-war identity and history, grappling with the national mythology of the

Third Reich'. Muddy paint and straw canvasses, sometimes placed behind life-size crashed warplanes, are not reflectively subtle!

It's not always clear, either, how (again in words from the Gagosian website):

> Anselm Kiefer's monumental body of work represents a microcosm of collective memory, visually encapsulating a broad range of cultural, literary, and philosophical allusions—from the Old and New Testaments, Kabbalah mysticism, Norse mythology and Wagner's Ring Cycle to the poetry of Ingeborg Bachmann and Paul Celan.

To me this feels a little pretentious: however relevant these sources and ideas are to the artist, it would often be hard for even an informed viewer to find references unless guided by essays, labels or tour guides. It feels like a kind of cultural namedropping, this alluding to such important texts and artists.

Anyway, the library books contained fascinating images of tunnels, stacked towers, a glasshouse full of hanging ribbons, vast industrial spaces filled with sculpture or left empty to emphasize their own sculptural forms. Without even reading the book I could see immediately themes of imprisonment, freedom, guilt, grief, hope, despair, ruins and renewal, all jumbled up and juxtaposed, clashing and yet connected.

My poem is an imaginary evocation of the site, but also a ventriloquist poem narrated by the sometimes fictional, sometimes actual, voice of the artist. The epigraph was used to frame the poem as questioning and doubting, with reference to Kiefer specifically but also the wider art world. What do we do when we conjure 'a bird' from studio bits and bobs? What is actually created? What are we seeing?

The first draft of my poem was almost in the stanza form it is now, with a diminishing number of lines as the poem proceeds, so I tidied it up. I'd like to claim it uses the symbolism of seven as a magical and alchemical number or the measure of planets, weekdays, and Egyptian paths to heaven, even of the Seven Heavenly Palaces written about by Jewish mystics and referred to by Kiefer, but I can't. It just happened.

I like the fact that Kiefer is happy to let people be confused and find their own route through his complex and their own connections between his works. I like that before one 'gets' or 'tries to understand' the work, there is the experience of the work itself, seen by the eyes, converted into language by the brain. In *My Way: Speeches and Poems* (University of Chicago Press, 1999) Charles Bernstein suggested that 'Poetry is turbulent thought, at least that's what I want from it.... It leaves things unsettled, unresolved—leaves you knowing less than you did when you started', something I have always clung to as a rationale for writing. And in this case it seems to chime with how Kiefer thinks and writes about his work.

That doesn't mean my poem is chaotic. It contains images, descriptions, but also associative and analogous ideas, a kind of meta-commentary perhaps imposed onto what can be 'seen'. Hopefully there is enough there for people to construct their own version of 'what the poem is about'. For me, there are ideas of hope in the lines about flight, the way ruins reveal traces of memory and the past (as in psychogeography and archaeology) to us in the present, and even in the final line, which is the kind of statement we should always interrogate, even wonder about. But I also accept what Anne Lauterbach said when interviewed for *What Is Poetry: Conversations with the American Avant-Garde* (Teachers & Writers Books, 2003): 'A poem is not a puzzle to be solved. A poem is an experience, an event, in and of language. It should be approached as such....'

Notes:

The Anselm Kiefer Foundation's website about Barjac is at https://eschaton-foundation.com/barjac/

The Gagosian artist's page for Kiefer is at https://gagosian.com/artists/anselm-kiefer/

Stuart Barnes

The White Rabbit's Tritina

after L. B.'s Stuart and Tinkerbell *(1998)*
for Z. H.

Witness the washing line's grace, the way the
boy———all chaotic halo———lifts me———white
as the Madonna's———to his face, rabbit

-hammered *Neu!* falling into place. Grab it,
his slick wingish collarbone, pillow the
surrealistic umbilicus———white

space wrinkles and riffles, shouts for joy. White
-tipped wand, he magicks every last drab bit
of Spain into Platja de Montgat's swathe.

Sketch. Trace the white lines. Wish. *Rabbit! Rabbit!*

in various ways as I wrote . White Rabbit.

was drilled into my head and came squirting out
It's byphonic. I've always been like this. Sketche

and I listened to it over and over for hours.

Davis' Sketches of Spain. I loved that album
One day we took acid and I put on Miles
march or bolero that builds in intensity.

came up with was based on a slow Spanish
that's ideal for my voice. The music I
I wrote the song in F-sharp minor, a key

How Grace Slick wrote . White Rabbit.

Notes:

Rotated and flipped text from Marc Myers' "How Jefferson Airplane's Grace Slick Wrote 'White Rabbit,'" *The Wall Street Journal*, May 31, 2016

Commentary

A few months ago, while procrastinating packing removalist boxes, I chanced upon a black-and-white portrait that L. B., a photographer-friend, took in 1998, when I was 19. In it, I'm wearing just got out of bed hair and Adidas trackpants, and cradling and gazing at Tinkerbell, a former goth housemate's pet white rabbit. Just out of shot is the flourishing basil we'd nibble daily. Larger than life, Tinkerbell was our North Melbourne home's center of attention, and well looked-after, but I wished for her to escape, to live freely, like *Watership Down*'s rabbits.

For many years I was unable to write about Tinkerbell – she arrived in my life when I felt overwhelmed by symptoms of rape-related PTSD and by the truly unconditional love of a man who encouraged me to reach out to a counsellor for the first time – "tears of joy and tears of sorrow," sings Bernard Sumner on New Order's 'Vanishing Point'.

Around the time of drafting 'The White Rabbit's Tritina' three albums were in heavy rotation—Miles Davis' *Sketches of Spain*, Siouxsie and the Banshees' *Through the Looking Glass*, Jefferson Airplane's *Surrealistic Pillow*. I recalled an interview with Grace Slick in the *Wall Street Journal* in which she talks about the relationship between her song 'White Rabbit', which closes *Surrealistic Pillow* and which was first performed with her previous band, The Great Society, and *Sketches of Spain*. I wanted to address this in the second half of 'The White Rabbit's Tritina' so I made a found poem using text from that interview. Here it is, in its original form:

How Grace Slick wrote 'White Rabbit'

I wrote the song in F-sharp minor, a key
that's ideal for my voice. The music I
came up with was based on a slow Spanish

march or *bolero* that builds in intensity.
One day we took acid and I put on Miles
Davis' *Sketches of Spain*. I loved that album

and I listened to it over and over for hours.
It's hypnotic. I've always been like this. *Sketches*
was drilled into my head and came squirting out

in various ways as I wrote 'White Rabbit'.

But 'How Grace Slick ...' seemed incomplete. I came
to realize that it needed to acknowledge Siouxsie and the
Banshees. The band named its record label Wonderland, after
Lewis Carroll's *Alice's Adventures in Wonderland*; its eighth
studio album, *Through the Looking Glass*, a collection of cover
versions, borrows its title from the novel's sequel. Second
track 'Hall of Mirrors', first recorded by Kraftwerk, includes
the lyrics 'Even the greatest stars / discover themselves in the
looking glass'. Aha! I rotated and flipped 'How Grace Slick ...'
– a tritina in appearance only – and, hey presto, generated its
hall of mirrors – and acid trip – vibe.

Written before the second half, the first half of 'The White
Rabbit's Tritina' is a traditional tritina, a form invented by Marie
Ponsot and Rosemary Deen. Its end-words are 'the', 'white' and
'rabbit', honoring Tinkerbell, Grace Slick and Siouxsie and the
Banshees/Kraftwerk/Lewis Carroll. Scaffold assembled, I was
almost ready to write, ethically, about Tinkerbell. What might
she (not) need / (not) want to say? I researched the zoological
and cultural histories, mythologies and folklores of rabbits. I'm
drawn to religious iconography and in the poem – dedicated to

a close friend, a supporter of Catalan Independence who lived in Montgat, Catalonia, when I wrote the poem – allude to a favourite painting, Titian's *The Madonna of the Rabbit*.

Forms like the tritina are 'instruments of discovery', says Marie Ponsot. 'They create an almost bodily pleasure in the poet. They are not restrictive. They pull things out of you'. 'The White Rabbit's Tritina' isn't a rape poem, but it illuminates my dissolution of my rape-related shame and my reshaped perceptions of my body and my body image. I view myself – and *Stuart* and *Tinkerbell* – through the lens of tenderness now.

Works Cited:

Marc Myers, "How Jefferson Airplane's Grace Slick Wrote 'White Rabbit,'" *The Wall Street Journal*, May 31, 2016.

Dinitia Smith, "Recognition at Last for a Poet of Elegant Complexity," *The New York Times*, April 13, 1999.

SUDEEP SEN

Disembodied

for Amitav Ghosh

1.

My body carved from abandoned bricks of a ruined temple,
                    from minaret-shards of an old mosque,
from slate-remnants of a medieval church apse,
        from soil tilled by my ancestors.

My bones don't fit together correctly   as they should –
the searing ultra-violet light from Aurora Borealis
            patches and etch-corrects my orientation –
magnetic pulses prove potent.

My flesh sculpted from fruits of the tropics,
                        blood from coconut water,
skin coloured by brown bark of Indian teak.

My lungs fuelled by Delhi's insidious toxic air
        echo asthmatic sounds, a new vinyl dub-remix.
Our universe – where radiation germinates from human follies,
            where contamination persists from mistrust,
where pleasures of sex are merely a sport –
where everything is ambition,
everything is desire,   everything is nothing.
                Nothing and everything.

2.

White light everywhere,
but no one can recognize its hue,
no one knows that there is colour in it – all possible colours.

Body worshipped, not for its blessing,
                but its contour –
                        artificial shape shaped by Nautilus.
Skin moistened by L'Oreal
        and not by season's first rains –
skeleton's strength not shaped by earthquakes
                or slow-moulded by fearless forest-fires.

Ice-caps are rapidly melting – too fast to arrest glacial slide.
In the near future – there will be no water left
or too much water that is undrinkable,
                        excess water that will drown us all.
Disembodied floats,   afloat like Noah's Ark –

no gps, no pole-star navigation,   no fossil fuel to burn away –
just maps with empty grids and names of places that might exist.

Already, there is too much traffic on the road –
unpeopled hollow metal-shells   without brakes,
swerve about   directionless –   looking for an elusive
        compass.

Disembodied: Within

for Aditi Mangaldas

You emerge – from *within* darkness, your face
                        sliding into light –
you squirm virus-like in a womb,
draped blood-red,   on black stage-floor.
                 Around you, others swirl about
dressed as green algae,
            like frenetic atoms
        under a microscope in a dimly lit laboratory.
Art mirroring life – reflecting the pandemic on stage.

Your hands palpitate,
            as the sun's own blinding yellow corona
cracks through the cyclorama.
          People leap about – masked, veiled.
                     You snare a man's sight
with your fingers mimicking a *chakravavyuh* –
        you are red, he is green, she is blue –
trishanku – life, birth, death –
        regermination, rejuvenation, nirvana.

Everything on stage – as in life –
                   moves in circular arcs.
Irises close and open, faces veiled unveil –
     hearts love, lungs breathe – breathless.

Lights, electromagnetic –   *knotted, unwrapped* –
                music pulsates, reaching a crescendo,
                                                then silence.
Time stops. Far away in the infinite blue of the cosmos –
                I look up and spot a moving white.
I see a white feather
                                trying its best to breathe
in these times of breathlessness, floating downwards –

and as it touches the floor, in a split-second
everything bursts into colour, movement, the *bols/taals*
                                        try to restore order,
rhythm,   both contained and free.

The backdrop bright orange,
                            the silhouettes pitch-black.
As you embrace another humanform,
            the *infinite journey of timelessness* might seem
                                        inter_rupted,
but now is the moment to reflect and recalibrate
immersed in the *uncharted seas,* in the *widening circles,*
                telling us –   others matter,
the collective counts.

I examine minutely the striated strands
                of the pirouetting feather, now fallen –
its heart still beating, its blood still pumping,
                                its white untarnished.

Life's dance continues – with or without us –
only in the understanding of what is,
is there freedom from what is.

Commentary

1.

In 'Disembodied', the Delhi skyscape and the polluted air provide the essential ekphrastic canvas for the poem. These in turn are mapped onto our own body's architecture. The changing colors of the atmosphere due to the effects of climate change, and the way that we and our bodies react to it – both external and internal – play a very important part. There is also idea of refraction in physics, allusion to Noah's Ark and Biblical/ancestral histories, the cyclical time and life cycles, the self-conscious attitude to beauty and body, the relentless reliance on speed and technology – all these provide the visual and artistic template from where I draw the inspiration for this poem.

Ultimately, the poem is about the seamless interplay between science and the arts, between elements in nature and humankind, between perception and deception, between words and images. Despite our intellect and logic, we are all 'directionless' at one level – 'looking for an elusive compass' to guide and sustain us.

2.

It was the singular startling image of a white feather falling from the imagined skies that caught my attention and kickstarted the poem 'Disembodied: Within'. This snapshot derives from a pivotal moment in Aditi Mangaldas's dance production, 'Within', where – after the high-speed freneticism of bodies moving swiftly in a choreographed manner with resounding music – everything stops still, everything freezes, and in the sudden still silence, you see a feather pirouette in the air falling downwards. 'And as it touches the floor, in a split-second / everything bursts into color, movement, the *bols/taals* / try to restore order, / rhythm, both contained and free'.

Often one cannot intellectually pinpoint the inspirational moment or justify why it happened at that very minute. The science (and art) of neural transmission is a fascinating area to study, one that I have delved a lot into. Classical dance and music have always been a source of inspiration for many of my ekphrastic poetms. In fact, the book I am currently working on, titled *The Whispering Anklets*, is entirely on this subject. The basis for all the poems in this book is based on the idea of ekphrasis.

Linda Black

I'm diving into him

My dead ex-husband (miniature, faintly winged, Abelard our cat – female – coiled on his head ...) and I don't have children (yet) – we're inside a void – my family's there too, individually cocooned in a thin skin – a vernix – protective, though they're not youngsters. My father's got his walking stick and he no longer works for Pathé News; my mother's in her rollers – or maybe I'm confusing her with an old illustration (unpublished) – a story written by a (then) friend (of ours) – metal wave-clips (with teeth), spotted pinafore, maybe a moustache (not really) ... Nanna (beloved/step)) – fishcakes with a bit of sugar, rhubarb pies, grandad with his pocket-watch.

There's plenty of others (un-beings) floating around – crossed legs seated on a cushion[1], gargoyles, distortions – festering, otherwise engaged ... floating, clumping, mingling, mangling, pointing a finger, bobbing, blabbing, clobbering, lobbing, leaning (a well-dressed lady on a smaller character's upper back – child maybe): demeaned, distorted, despicable, detrimental, disagreeable, wonky, wavering, other worldly, stressed, stipulated, reaching out. Very fine.

I've just looked and they're further away, my family, over the other side from where we/he are/is (perched on the stump of a tree) – Grandad's got his hat on, my father's sideways wearing braces, his arthritic legs scribbled out; Nanna's in slippers, that crossover apron; my mother, in a hairnet, flabby belly nothing but her roll-on on, a star of David around her neck....

For protection.

No depiction of my (tiny) little sister.

1. Mistake – elsewhere, in a different void.

Commentary

From an early poem entitled 'Artwork':

> She begins without an idea:
> a freshly grounded etching plate, hard
> and unblemished. The first mark she makes
> is not in an obvious place, central say,
> or two thirds down, it merely is, as though
> it has landed from the sky.

My tutor at Art School, Robin Page – a member of the Fluxus group of artists, told me once that where I began on a page was unusual – 'not central or two-thirds down' – and in a way he gave me my originality.

'I'm diving into him' is from a manuscript of ekphrastic poems relating to my own artwork/processes. Its focus is an early copperplate etching, nameless, just a number. At this time I hadn't begun or anticipated writing (the flipside of the same coin).

For the poem, I chose a particular section, focusing on a very small (nude) figure, my representation of my former husband. This time I knew/had known I was drawing him, our cat, myself, likewise my parents and grandparents, though, within the tumult of multiple floating 'beings', I have no idea where I began, who or what those others may be/have been.

I drew into the blackened wax ground with a fine sewing needle in a holder, working spontaneously, attentive to detail. One of the wonders of etching, an intaglio printmaking process, is that the image is reversed when printed (some artists, including Rembrandt, use/used a mirror whilst drawing), thus the resulting image is seen anew. For this I like it all the more.

As with the execution of the etching, I began the poem with a spontaneous first line not knowing or wanting to know the outcome, a process I have learnt to trust. When I first began writing prose poetry some years ago, I didn't know what it was – I'd been looking at a cut-down/diminished door in my home, and the thought 'I like this door' popped into my mind – I decided to write it down. Thus followed a prose meditation on the door. I took it to a workshop run by Mimi Khalvati, for whom I have much gratitude. She told me it was a perfect example of a prose poem. I came to love the form – how, as with a Rembrandt etching, there is precision, fine detail, though the edges disappear into the ether, thus opening it out.

Despite having a reference, I worked from my memory of the image, not the actual image (see the note at the end of the poem) – a matter of fancy, inclination, trust in the process. Nor do I censor – later, a bit of editing.

I began – as I often do, on an impulse. Why I thought of this particular etching I do not know; I may have been thinking of the void (as I do), the lack of ground, foundation, boundaries. A frame (not that this print is framed) does not really contain, nor does it cut off what lies beyond. It is the open-endedness that appeals, the floating who knows where, as the/my mind is, as it were, uncontained, unstill – writhing. The poem became symbolic of my passing life – the lost ones – my inner life, machinations, incredulity, my sadness and sorrow.

I allow words to take on their own life, venture forth uncensored, sound and meaning combined, and I let them be.

PAUL MUNDEN

The Memory of an Angel
after Alban Berg Violin Concerto: soloist Nigel Kennedy, 1990

We've only just settled
when we're appalled

by the curious apparition
that shambles onstage

in long black cloak
and ghostly make-up

that accentuates the rough
love-bite on his neck,

kiss or curse
of the wooden appendage

now clamped between
collarbone and chin

as our applause –
for who knows what – dies

down and he starts tuning up,
or so it seems – the open

strings so commonplace,
so quiet – but it's the pulse

of haunting, musical life
from which a masterpiece

will emerge, and what we hear
comes not from a score

but flowing from the soul
via the muscular

chambers of the heart
like spontaneous

pleasure – and pain, unforeseen
by both the child in the story

and the childlike violin-man
who bears witness

to her tragic paralysis
and premature demise,

the composer's grief
a long moment of almost

deafening dissonance,
our empathy intense

as each solemn accomplice
seated behind the soloist

follows their part like fate
and with unerring belief.

A Carinthian folk tune
drifts in as if from afar

or that other country, the past,
like lost innocence.

Equally distant is the ethereal
chorale, the premonition

of every funeral
we will ever have to bear.

What is memory without
loss? And what would we make

of loss without memory?
How else would we create

such immaculate silence
as follows this performance,

every member of the audience
held in thrall?

The black cloak is both pall
and the dress of a dark angel.

As he bows out, he taps his fist
against his pounding chest.

Commentary

In 1990, Nigel Kennedy played the Berg Violin Concerto in a concert for the 'BBC at 60'. The concerto memorializes Manon Gropius, daughter of Alma Mahler, to whom Berg had been very close. The performance was by all accounts sublime, but also controversial: Kennedy chose to wear a black cloak and ghostly make-up. John Drummond, then Controller of BBC Radio 3, was outraged. Who, though, was more justified, the performer or the critic? In my poem I explore both the performance and the audience reaction; the poignancy of the music and the drama of the event. In this commentary I provide further information about the concerto that puts Kennedy's approach to the work in some context.

Manon died having suffered infantile paralysis from polio, aged eighteen. Described by her mother as 'a creative energy, such as I have never seen' (in Haste 2019: 249), she was allowed to go around naked. For the conductor Bruno Walter she was 'an unearthly apparition' (306). Carl Zuckmayer, playwright, gave her snakes, for which she had a passion. After Manon's death, Berg wrote, 'I can no longer live without her ... I want to travel to Venice – put myself in her poor bed and open the gas tap' (312). Turning his desperation to more creative resolve, he composed a requiem in the form of a violin concerto, written at his summer cottage beside the Wörthersee in Carinthia, between May and August 1935. While there, Berg suffered a serious insect bite and died of blood poisoning a few months later. As Alma Mahler commented, the requiem for her child effectively became his own.

It's a complex work. It uses the twelve-note tone-row system developed by Schoenberg, which has scope for producing extreme dissonance, but Berg combines that with more traditional harmonic elements. It incorporates both a Carinthian folk song and a Bach chorale ('Es ist genug') – one that Kennedy was familiar with from his Sunday singing sessions at the Menuhin School, and one of his favorites. There are textual descriptions in the score – 'groans', 'cries' – indications of how the music relates to its story.

Berg is considered an expressionist, a term explained well by Donald J. Grout: 'The subject matter of expressionism is man as he exists in the modern world ... isolated ... prey to inner conflict ... and all the elemental irrational drives of the subconscious, and in irritated rebellion against established order and accepted forms' (1973: 706). This description has an uncanny resemblance to Kennedy himself, performing the Berg concerto. But instead of marveling at such an embodiment of the music, John Drummond – representing the established order – chose to publicly denounce it.

Drummond even suggested that the red patch of skin on Kennedy's neck, a common affliction among violinists, was some kind of Dracula allusion. Like 'a misplaced extra for the *Rocky Horror Show*', wrote Stephen Johnson (n.d.), and to be fair, Kennedy's make-up perhaps accentuated the love-bite look, but the idea of the visual effect trivializing the music – the same type of accusation levelled against Ken Russell's films – is too *easy*. Russell's *Mahler* of 1974 may seem 'over the top' – Gustav has visions of himself in a glass coffin; Cosima Wagner appears in pseudo Nazi dress – but its dramatic purpose is sincere. As Jonathan Dakss (n.d.) comments, it's a film where 'historical content matters less than metaphors, feelings, emotions, and interpretations'; the style of the film is scrupulously honest about those priorities. And 'sensational', lurid imagery is not always far-fetched. There can be genuine grounds for its relevance. Consider Manon's extreme theatricality – and Berg's, envisioning himself committing suicide *in Manon's bed*. Some have identified an even darker side to the composer, and Chris Walton describes Berg's drawings as 'what one might expect to see scribbled by a thirteen-year-old boy on the back of a school toilet door'. One of them 'depicts a naked woman ... heavily pregnant ... striding with open legs toward a man in soldier's uniform with a dagger at his belt, who is holding toward her what is either the hilt of a knobbly-ended sword or a highly elongated, erect, black penis' (Walton 2014: 81).

And Russell is 'over the top'? Kennedy 'inappropriate'? Berg's concerto may be dedicated 'Dem Andenken eines Engels' ('to the memory of an angel') but Berg was also a sexual obsessive, with some Nazi sympathies. If, as rumored, Kennedy really wanted to have a blood capsule in his mouth, only persuaded against that at the last minute, I for one am tempted to forgive him.

As Kennedy puts it, the concerto 'is all about redemption after the destruction of the body' (in Doggett 1996: 132); redemption of a sort for Manon, but also redemption for the miscreant Berg. My poem seeks redemption for Kennedy too.

Marc Vincenz

Artisanal

But we worshipped the artists who made noise out of nothing, who brought light out of the dark, who shared the intimate knowledge of their souls, who appeared in the mind as a peach or a pear, who could fly above the clouds and remain there, who sensed how to love, even in the darkest corner of the building.

Commentary

"Artisanal" is about people living in a society who need something to carry them through. These people are in awe of artists who, from nothing, create something interesting that is unknown prior to this moment. In essence, it is about art saving civilization because, without art, civilization cannot endure. When I talk about art, I am talking about it in the larger scheme of things, from dance to painting to poetry to jazz—whatever we create. These are the things that make life worth living, especially outside of the epicurean. Of course, great food is art, too. But it also helps you get through the day knowing you will have something delicious on the table. And the same thing can be said about poetry or painting or dance or music. It's what helps you get through life. If we didn't have these things—amazing food, great art and even great sex— what would make life worth living? It is the beginning of beauty.

Artist Jake Quatt has created etchings for my book, *Coalition Number Nine*, from which this prose poem is taken.

Moira Egan

M

an exploded sestina

She's nude but for the bestial pelt of hair
that cataracts, thick gold and red;
cascades around her breasts, leaving them bare.
The perfect amphiboly of her gaze
of ecstasy and pain in equal parts.
One hand protects her heart.

Theatrically she clutches at her heart.
Her gown is golden luscious, but her hair
is frazzled, as if rent, as if this part
is not quite done; relinquishing the red,
the madder, ruddled soul of sin. That gaze
(within, without) leaves her completely bare.

Although she's richly clothed she wears a bare
expression of despair. The maudlin heart.
Her head's inclined; her earthward-facing gaze
inscrutable; the uncombed strands of hair.
A single tear; her face is splotched with red.
Perfume; a strand of pearls that's come apart.

The graceful fingers, held apart,
to prise the jar of unguent. Bare
and clear the myrrh and frankincense, a red
and black olfaction. Necklace at her heart;

so much in shadow: velvet bodice, hair.
Is that a smile? or dark and downcast gaze?

(And you: don't frame yourself within that gaze
                    nor come apart;
            and never rend your hair
                              nor bare
your barren heart.
Utter red,
                    blood red
        the bloodshot gaze,
                ever more weary the heart
        you've learned to hold apart,
ever more bare.
        And you: never let down your hair.)

Commentary

I collect Magdalenes. I don't just mean that I collect the postcards of the Magdalenes that I've seen, though I mean that too. Titian, Artemisia, Caravaggio, Benson Ambrosius. When I walk into an overwhelming Church or Museum or Villa, my gaze takes me straight to whatever Magdalene may be on display. Then she remains in my memory.

> mag·da·lene | ˌmagdaˈlēn | (also magdalen)
> noun
> (the Magdalen or the Magdalene) St. Mary Magdalene.
> ✦ archaic a reformed prostitute.
> ✦ archaic a home for reformed prostitutes.
> ORIGIN: late Middle English: via ecclesiastical Latin from Greek (Maria hē) Magdalēnē '(Mary of) Magdala' (to whom Jesus appeared after his resurrection; John 20:1–18), formerly identified with the sinner of Luke 7:37.

What a subject. On the one hand, she's sexy beyond belief, the gains of her "BC" life as a prostitute richly paintable, fully on display. Her long, luscious locks; her dress, silk or velvet in all the shades of red; pearls (of wisdom?); her characteristic alabaster jar of unguent. Her delicate and skillful hands. A painter's dream.

OR: penitent, pious, one of the unsung disciples of Christ. Eyes downcast. Ripped, rent; her hair a red and ratty mess, prefiguring even Lady Godiva's long-hair dress. Even so, every so often, a nipple peeks coyly through. Here she's abject, skin and bones; in another medium, Donatello's jagged sculpture comes to mind. Rags and crags and sorrow.

Sorrow. Maudlin: "*late Middle English (as a noun denoting*

Mary Magdalen): from Old French Madeleine, from Church Latin Magdalena. The current sense derives from allusion to pictures of Mary Magdalen weeping."

I think one reason that, as a poet, I'm drawn to Magdalene is that she is a perfect embodiment of Keats' concept of *negative capability*. Keats believed that one of the key attributes of the poetic mind is that it is "capable of being in uncertainties, Mysteries, doubts, without any irritable reaching after fact and reason." Magdalene is a figure who utterly embodies a sense of dichotomy, not least that famous dichotomy known as the Madonna-Whore Complex. (Although, admittedly, in this case it's more complicated, as, no matter what, the Magdalene is contradistinct to the "real" Madonna, that other woman grieving at the base of the cross, the one dressed in blue, not red. *Stabat mater*, the mother of the man for whom they have torn their garments, rent their hair.)

Mother of, lover of. I'll confess: having grown up in the 1970s, *Jesus Christ Superstar* is one of the great touchstones of my adolescence. Sometimes I pull up a video on YouTube and, no matter which song it is, I know all the words, all the background bops and drops, all the nuances. "So if you are the Christ ..." or "Peter, don't you know what you have said ..." or, most relevant and heart-tugging of all, "I don't know how to love him / what to do, how to move him ..."

That last, of course, is Mary Magdalene, singing of her love for Jesus, decades before Dan Brown took us down that road of Magdalene as chief apostle/lover/common-law wife of Christ. "And I've had so many men before / in very many ways / he's just one more."

Let us not forget that Yvonne Elliman, the actress who played that version of Mary Magdalene, went on to have a number-one disco hit with the classic, "If I Can't Have You." What a wonderful intertextual conundrum, these songs, that singer: "If I can't have you, I don't want nobody, baby." I'm in love with Jesus Christ, who's about to die on the cross for my sins.

What a way to inform an adolescent Catholic girl's imagination: sex and sin, desire and despair, body and soul. Is it any wonder my eye goes straight to that auburn-haired figure, chiaroscuroed in the corner? Is it any wonder I've spent years and lines and rhymes trying to make sense of why she means so much to me? "Don't you think it's rather funny / I should be in this position ..."

Or is it? Magdalene, it is said, was the first to see the resurrected Christ, having rolled the stone away from his tomb, that second chapter of his *incarnation*.

Incarnation: "(especially of a deity or spirit) embodied in flesh; in human form: *God incarnate | he chose to be incarnate as a man.*" And what is it that we as poets do? We embody abstract ideas and feelings in concrete, even visceral images.

Images. Imagine. Imagination. Magic. Think of the Magi, bringing gifts. Think of poetry as gift and sacrament. Think of Magdalene, sacramentally, anointing him with unguent. Think of a poem, from the Greek, *poiima*—a made thing, a thing made of stuff. We make our poems out of, well, such stuff as dreams are made on, but we translate these dreams into symbols, into meaning-making machines that translate what we want to say to our readers. Translate, after all, comes from the Latin, basically, to carry over. Metaphor comes from the Greek, basically, to transfer, to carry over.

Beyond metaphor, maybe it's even a little meta: my obsession with Mary Magdalene, she who bows down, she who gazes up, she who earthily anoints us with what is holy. With humility. With love. With language.

[definitions from the little Merriam-Webster that resides in my computer]

Dominique Hecq

The Doors

The regulating line is a guarantee against wilfulness
—Le Corbusier

i.

The house rocks like a boat tugging at its moorings. Inner weather, gusty. We're playing dead fish. Mike Parr's *Head on a Plate* regards me. I stare back. I'm gone with the wind, gills and fins fluttering. Disappear the golden orb spinning its silk threads in cirrus clouds branching against the sky. Unstick myself from the idea of arachnophobia and away from the viscid spiral of sticky thread joining windowpane to Parr's etching. The head is distorted. I disappear the shadowed eye sockets. Squint. With a slight adjustment of perspective, I catch sight of an anamorphic skull: punKtime. Death brushes past. We are *The Ambassadors* now, waiting for Godot. Maestro strides in through the lounge's butter doors. Opens the baby grand's lid. Fingers scurry on the keyboard. Hammers hammer strings. The floorboards shake. Walls are reefs. I'm a jellyfish. Starfish. Rock fish. A rolling stone that doesn't know what it sways. *God, ready?* Nose aloft, the dog holds my gaze. *Roll. Left. Right. Left. Right. Turn and toss.* Fur and silk ripple. Passage of blazing light as backdrop. Melting butter. We are The Doors now. Heterodogsia, unsinging the dance. Körperbild. *People are Strange, my dog. Rock!*

ii.

At night, when silence trembles with echoes and moonshine bobs on the floorboards casting shards of shadows on the walls, we leave them open to the dark, the doors. To terrorise the Architect who looks down upon this phantom world *in ille tempore*. Because all life holds its own destruction and God is nothing but the arbitrary distinction between heaven and earth, left and right, margin and immargination. Cut, not suture. Kinetic poesis. No beginning, but rhythm, repetition, spacing, caesura: difference from self. Dog centre. Repercussion, resonance, reverberation, resounding, revenance, reflection, return from within difference. Humans or otherwise, we are constituted by rhythm. This caesura sentence which gathers and segments and which means that every single thing can be danced like a prose poem unleashing the rules of lexis, grammar, syntax. In ruffle reef light, fur and silk ripple and brush. *Time is paradoxical … it folds or twists; it is as various as the dance of flames in a brazier, here interrupted, there vertical, mobile and unexpected.* Because we are truly fickle matter existing. Already exiting. Rocking the boat to the breath of time.

Commentary

A prose poem in two parts, 'The Doors' addresses literally and metaphorically the theme of this anthology. It explores and explodes Le Corbusier's aphorism chosen as epigraph, "The regulating line is a guarantee against wilfulness," through a multiplicity of ekphrastic maneuvers.

Rather than looking at architecture as a frame, framework or object defined in spatial terms, I approach it from the inside out as lived in *timespace* to evoke a real irreal event that bypasses rational cognition. Past the threshold commonly called doorstep, we enter the outer chambers of the heart through the two yellow doors of the living room. This space is inviolable and open to experimentation in real life, fostering an imaginary conversation across the arts through associative and aleatory processes which are subliminal and topokinetic. We also enter the body's inner chambers lined with doubt, disobedience and defiance by way of sound-images, proto-structures, lexicon-leaps which all erupt surreptitiously in a blazing dance between an animal and a human. The piece is in two parts to enhance its reflexive and ironic *retournement* which is also a *détournement*. Indeed, the deployment of multiple ekphrastic maneuvers hijacks prose poetry only to return it as stripped of generic specificity at the confluence of mute eloquence and philosophy.

Like dance and composition, architecture depends for its existence on things outside itself: time, people, money, craft, politics, ethics, mess. It may also depend on other arts such as painting and sculpture – even music. Hence, despite claims to the autonomy, purity and control that architects often make about their practice, contingency rocks architecture.

Circumstances invariably interfere with plans and schedules – not least time and weather. Also note that the French word 'temps' denotes both time and weather.

The point of contact between architecture, dance and poetry is time. More specifically rhythm, for rhythm impels movement. Time: immediate, multiple, connected ... or not; linear, cyclical, collective ... or subjective. 'The Doors' crosses the threshold of personal time, its multiplicity and interconnectedness. It considers the instant explosion of an event in part one and its temporal arc in part two. Here space is temporalized: the house is a real house where people make music and sculptures, scribble and design buildings, dance and invent computer games. In it hangs Mike Parr's original *Head on a Plate*. The Doors' 'People Are Strange' wafts wordless through real air in real time. The dance between a real dog and a fake dancer who replays the song's words in her mind also occur in real time. That is before committing the experience to paper in surreal mode.

Ekphrasis: from the Greek *ek* / *out* and *phrasis* /*speak*. The verb *ekphrazein* means to call an inanimate object by name.

Leo Spitzer famously defines ekphrasis as "the poetic description of a pictorial or sculptural work of art, which implies, in the words of Théophile Gauthier, 'une transposition d'art', the reproduction, through the medium of words, of sensuously perceptible objets d'art' (1955: 72). Spitzer's oft quoted definition highlights the dialectical struggle between the visual and the verbal at the heart of what may be called a classical understanding of ekphrasis, one that still pervades poetics to this day.

Ekphrasis remains a genre inherently fraught with tension even as it pushes the limits of its field of practice. We are dealing with meta-representations in which the verbal contains glosses, frames, or fixes the visual or plastic (sometimes aural) in a language of interpretation and displacement. It need not be so. As Cassandra Atherton and Paul Hetherington remind us, the contemporary practice of ekphrasis is more constricted than it was in ancient Greece (Atherton & Hetherington 2017).

Approaching writing 'The Doors', I set about to return ekphrasis to its original meaning through upsetting binaries, hierarchies and rhythms. I focused on dogged waywardness and defiance of the Architect with a number of questions and incipient answers: What are the margins of ekphrasis? What is a verbal representation of a visual representation? Can it be aural, too? Olfactive? This is the stuff of the dream work of the text. A carrying over from one code or sign system to another towards a transposition of lived experience whose drive to ek would yield a 'biographeme' (Barthes 1981: 42). And why not an *autographeme*?

And how does ekphrasis speak to us in the twenty-first century as 'the practice of glossing one mode of expression with another mode' (Gibson 2014) across time, space, medium, genre and language? Across myth and ideology. Could I gesture towards imagined futures from the sacred to the agnostic, mimesis to abstract expressionism, representation to presentation, academicism to in(ter)ventive praxis as one of *The Ambassadors* now waiting for Godot?

Works Cited:

Atherton, Cassandra & Hetherington, Paul, 'Poetry that sees', *Cordite* 51 (2017): 1 https://cordite.org.au/essays/ekphrastic-editorial [accessed 04.05.2023]

Barthes, Roland, *Camera Lucida: Reflections on Photography*, trans. Richard Howard. (New York: Hill & Wang, 1981), p. 42.

Gibson, Ross, 'Self extraction,' in Shane Strange, Hetherington, Paul, & Webb, Jen (eds.), *Creative Manoeuvres: Writing, Making, Being* (Newcastle-Upon-Tyne: Cambridge Scholars Publishing, 2014), pp. 1-17.

Le Corbusier, *Towards a New Architecture* (USA: CPSIA, n. d.), p. 3.

Serres, Michel & Latour, Bruno, *Conversations on Science, Culture, and Time.* Ed. Roxanne Lapidus (Ann Arbor: University of Michigan Press, 1995), p. 58.

Spitzer, Leo, *Essays on English and American Literature,* ed. Anna Hatcher (Princeton: Princeton University Press, 1955), p. 89.

JESSICA L. WILKINSON

Appalachian Spring

Every force evolves a form
—Shaker proverb

I gained the ledge
—Hart Crane, *The Bridge*

1.

A simple fence structures the field
of the stage
as eight figures file through a bone-frame
threshold
signal poise   signal gratitude   signal hope
against internment lines
what fortune will emerge   a steady stream
of rising triads
opens onto pastoral plains   creeping
westward
over Susquehanna River   over Allegheny
Mountains
a dominant chord hovers   over
the tonic
to light a mythic American Dream

2.

A shift in posture starts a two-beat
rhythmic motif for a farmhouse
dialogue on tension and release:

> two palms firm in prayer
   or cupped and clapping at the soil;   Human
> hands at work to stitch and sow   =   Bodies
   or clasped in patience, faith;   Sound
> hold one's fluttering heart   Design
   or bang pans for mock charivari

Divergent energies gather at the seams
of national demands. Rock becomes step
becomes pulpit; bench becomes pew.

3.

The story elongates the bodies of men—saw, measuring tool,
   athlete.
To be hybrid anticipates the future. The story makes women
   multiple—
planted earth, devotee, sunbeams shaken overhead. Husband
   and bride
in parallel motion, drawn into the quiet space. The story is
   about two
palms meeting, or arms gripped at the elbow. The story
   expands beyond
picket-lines. No Shakers on Pennsylvania soil, yet *movement
   never lies.*

4.

Bassoon bounding motion secured by a planted toe:

Copland conducts a pack of horses into Hollywood
Technicolor; they follow on flute, long skirts lifted
on ankles to giddy-up across dry dirt   A circlet of
faithful energy leads a man to water: to sip, to stray

The matriarch drags her body across an intervening contour.

5.

Prick shoulders. Fold sky into ground, fidelity into kitchen. Spin
and defer. Wash and wag. Press into earth. Angular vocabulary
draws into the muscle's core while presto lines extract many-
storied gestures from the subconscious—a movement system,
gaining traction as American dance method. Graham's bride
evolves on time.

6.

Noguchi chose to enter the camps at Poston.
His fevered, hybrid dream—bodies breathing
around a shape build resistance to 'empty' or
'full': woodland refuge barricade speedway

7.

Rondo on daily activities of husband   wife
instruments of spring
                        widen into A   whirl into S

There will be disappointments   interrupting registers
point   sting   genuflect | mediate   well wish
        seeds of scored suspense cliché

Symbolic markers console other truths
duress of a nation   a shape to estrange
The chair   a tool   a bed   a cradle   stirs   *America* beyond

8.

blessed lessons done

turned back so as to less

blindly see the couple, left

alone   flecks of Whistler

Wood   outshaded by sunset

on eternal harmony

Commentary

In 1942 modern dancer and choreographer Martha Graham approached composer Aaron Copland to write music for an American-themed ballet. They had a back-and-forth about possible scenarios and tentatively agreed upon Graham's script called "House of Victory", set during the Civil War. In a gesture of support for America's involvement in World War II, Graham wanted to draw parallels between the abolishment of slavery in the historical war with the fight against Nazism. In response to the score that she received, however, Graham revised the scenario so that the original narrative was much more abstracted—the performance follows one day in the life of a newlywed pioneer couple, who convey their hopes and fears; they are offered lessons for steering through difficult times from both an older pioneer woman and an impassioned preacher, while a flock of four female followers remind the couple of the community resources available to them as they build their life together.

While I have always found it difficult to warm to Graham's style (I was raised on classical ballet and was more a fan of Balanchine's dynamism), I am intrigued by her desire to forge an authentically "American" dance movement, rather than to impose European methods on her dancers. Contrary to the ethereal "weightless" imperative of classical ballet, Graham emphasized the body as angular, dramatic, and grounded on the earth by laws of gravity. Building upon the ideas of performer and teacher Francois Delsarte, who understood the expressions and gestures of the body to be manifestations of inner emotions or states of mind, Graham's style developed from the interplay between the contraction or tensing of a muscle and the flow that emanated from the release or relaxing of that tension. She also explored the body's percussive potential through falling to the floor, or weighted steps, or sometimes through striking the floor or legs. The characters in *Appalachian Spring* express their inner thoughts and feelings through this movement vocabulary, and we can interpret the symbolism—as the husband widens his stance repeatedly into an A shape, for example, we see him "expanding" into the open prairies of the so-called "New World", or, he is testing the limits of his strength and stamina.

Copland, too, had been looking to throw off European influences in his development of an American "vernacular" style, turning to folk music as one way to find textures and harmonies of such a localized quality. His compositions such as *Fanfare for the Common Man* (1942) or *Lincoln Portrait* (1942) contain origin strands that we have come to associate with a kind of quintessential, "patriotic" American sound. Indeed, that sound is echoed within Hollywood film scores, often of the war or adventure variety, such as *Saving Private Ryan, Superman* or *Apollo 13*. Copland's sonic textures and open harmonies were associated with the vast American landscape and hardy pioneer spirit. *Appalachian Spring* exhibits its own "American" symbolism from the opening bars—Copland refers to but subverts traditional functional harmony, building up a polyharmony instead; this might be interpreted as a symbol of the mythic American Dream, where democracy and opportunity emerge out of a break with tradition.

The most striking component of the performance, in my opinion, is the set design, by Japanese-American artist Isamu Noguchi. These non-literal and minimalist sets are reminiscent of Noh theatre designs—simple wooden structures represent an entrance way, a bench, a rock, a house with steps and a chair, and a fence; each appear as if whittled to the bare bones. Annagret Fauser refers to Noguchi's designs here as a response to racial hostility within his own country; indeed, when he created the sets for *Appalachian Spring*, he had only just been released from detention in Poston's internment camp for Japanese Americans during the war. Blending Western modernism with Japanese art, Noguchi explored the possibilities of "artistic hybridity" (and by extension, hybrid identity) as an "American contribution to world culture" (Fauser, 43). Also intriguing about the sets and props is that our understanding of what they signify "transforms" as the dancers move around them—the rock at the back of the stage becomes a pulpit for the preacher; the outside bench becomes a church pew for the flock of worshippers; the chair becomes a cradle for the wife to imagine motherhood, and so on.

In their respective contributions to *Appalachian Spring*, Graham, Copland and Noguchi exhibit something of their individual attempts to explore and define a distinctly American art form, inflected with their own experiences. Yet the interplay between movement, objects and music in the performance resists solidifying into clichéd, homogenized Americana. We are drawn into the imagined space it creates; our interpreting minds do not simply receive a historical narrative essence but question the foundation of a nation's mythologies and ponder the multitudinous and diverse hands that have energized its current state.

Works Cited:

Annagret Fauser, *Aaron Copland's Appalachian Spring*, Oxford UP, 2017.

With thanks to Nicholas Bochner for his discussions about Copland's score.

Quotes within the poem:

"To be hybrid anticipates the future" – Isamu Noguchi
"Movement never lies" – Martha Graham

Toby Fitch

Let's Dance Redux

it wasn't Stravinsky's rite of spring to
plonk Uluru on his album cover
but it led a bleach-blond Bowie to the pub
summer dance-off & to his
echoing guitar riff in the video clip

da da-da-da da-da-da

becoming the rattle of the sheep truck
around dust-pink Carinda shops
the analogue wood clock
rewinding itself from the ground up
into an Elder's arms

da da-da-da da-da-da

becoming the nonchalance of the scowl
on the Brixton star's face
showing up race for what it is in Oz
while some old mate does the chicken wing
on chequered floors

da da-da-da da-da-da

becoming the trembling of a flower
over red rock formations

the digital mushroom cloud ghost of Maralinga
a jangling of AMEXed jewelry and the
working nightmare of lugging machines

da da-da-da da-da-da

in broad daylight scrubbing pavers
the tourist-y vista up Sydney Harbour's guts
all haze & helicopters
the desert guitar solo in baggy white pants
and yet none of this well-meaning

da da-da-da da-da-da

fetish for Aussie kitsch
could ever eclipse young Joelene's joy
stomping those high-heeled
red shoes blues
however much it wanted to

Commentary

'Let's Dance Redux' takes the music video for David Bowie's song 'Let's Dance' (1983) as its subject, and is mostly a homage for its, at the time, groundbreaking positive representation of Indigenous Australian issues in a pop cultural context. The poem begins with a separate ekphrastic moment, that of Bowie's interest in Australian iconography – the inspiration for the music video. As a boy, he was fascinated by an image of Uluru on the cover of Stravinsky's *The Rite of Spring:* 'The first time I had seen [Uluru] was on the cover of a Stravinsky album [...] It's a childhood image that stays in your mind, and it became an ambition of some kind'. That cover image led presumably to Bowie's obsession with Australia (he toured many times and kept an apartment near Sydney Harbour for several years), to the idea of staging a music video in the Australian outback, and to an awareness of Australia's ongoing racism since colonization – the genocides, the stolen unceded land, and subjugation of its Indigenous peoples. Bowie described the video (and the video for his subsequent single, 'China Girl', also filmed in Australia) as 'very simple, very direct' statements against racism and oppression, but also an unabashed statement about integration of one culture with (or into) another. It's this latter prerogative that 'Let's Dance Redux' eventually and gently critiques – the video's a classic, and it's fun, queer, tongue-in-cheek and well-meaning, but at the same time is perhaps hindered by its fetishization of Aussie iconography and kitsch. The poem, as with traditional ekphrases, is a description—in this case of the staccato, digitally delayed guitar riff and chord progression ('*da da-da-da da-da-da*'), and then of the imagery in the music video, moving chronologically, scene to scene: the town of Carinda and the pub scene showing awkward locals versus Bowie's upstandingness; the Aboriginal protagonists of the clip, Joelene King and Terry Roberts, oscillating between dancing and slaving away; the evocations of nuclear test site Maralinga; postcard shots of Sydney and its consumerism; a corny guitar solo set in the desert; and the image of Joelene and Terry treading on the red shoes she is made to wear to 'dance the blues' (whose blues?). Was it Bowie's or the director David Mallett's thought to have them do that, or was it Joelene's and Terry's improvised response to the imperative that they and their people integrate into the white English star's video clip and its settler representation of racism? I like to think it was the latter, a smiling subversion, stomping the materialistic red shoes into the ground, into country.

JONATHAN PENTON

Large Pulcinella

Sorel Etrog
Canadian, born in Romania, 1933
Large Pulcinella, 1965–67
Bronze
Gift of Sydney and Walda Besthoff, 99.132
Installation funded by William and Jane O'Malley

This lockdown
is
the point.

My blade
is one
with my crossguard.

The guard
is hopelessly
twisted.

This frustration
is more than
a symptom.

Commentary

I've been working on an ekphrastic project in the Sydney and Walda Besthoff Sculpture Garden, colloquially known as the New Orleans Sculpture Garden. There are a great number of nudes here, mostly of men, with carefully realized penises at rest. There are nudes of women, to be sure, and large detailed sculptures of vulvas. There are no erect penises, however. There are half-a-dozen obelisks, pointed at the sky, but all of them are fictionalized, symbol-laden, corrupted into something meaningful. It is my casual and biased observation that a vulva is art for its own sake, but a sculpture of an erect penis has to *mean* something.

One such meaningful penis at the New Orleans Sculpture Garden is *Large Pulcinella* by Sorel Etrog. Interesting for its inclusion of testicles, this phallus strikes me as being particularly unhappy, however engorged. The intricate lockwork at its base seems actively unkind. I imagined it cleaved the phallus from both purpose and desire. The detail on the erection itself began to seem like scar tissue, and the sculpture's odd head began to cry a dissatisfaction that transcended pain. I imagined the penis's consciousness had become inseparable from that pain, until it identified itself by its lockwork rather than its thrusting shape.

Leo Boix

A Latin American Sonnet LXXXI

In the famous engraving by artist Joaquín Torres García
América invertida, South America appears upside down
as an ill shaped and distorted supercontinent like Pangaea,
with the Andes facing West, and the pole turned around.
There's a frigate heading to Uruguay, a childish breeze,
a big sun on the coast of Argentina, a moon with six stars.
The Equator is now far South, and the Isthmus squeezed
like a yarará snake. America inverted in the shape of a guitar.
There are echoes of a pre-Columbian past, cosmic elements,
coordinates to break away from the North, a rising Tiwanaku[1]
looking in a modern direction, a beacon, a bold experiment
of liberation, a flipped cosmology, a laboratory of the new.
There, a streamlined manifesto for a South American youth.
His ink on paper drawing of 1943. 'Our North is the South'.

---

1. The spiritual and political center of the Tiwanaku culture. The capital of
a powerful pre-Hispanic empire that dominated a large area of the southern
Andes and beyond, reaching its apogee between 500 and 900 AD.

Commentary

I was always fascinated by the work and ideas of Uruguayan-Spanish artist, sculptor, muralist, novelist, writer, teacher, and theorist Joaquín Torres García (1874–1949), considered by many as the father of Latin American Constructivism. His seminal work *América Invertida*, a 1943 pen and ink drawing, features a depiction of South America that has been turned from its standard representation and is instead oriented with the South at the top. It includes child-like images of a fish, a boat, a moon and stars, and a rising sun. The drawing challenges socio-political notions of the North/South axis and questions U.S. cultural imperialism and the legacies of European colonization of the Americas. It also proposes a new art influenced by the traditions of the indigenous Americans, from the Mayas and Aztecs to the Incas, Guaranis and Mapuches. This artwork, which has become a central part of Uruguayan popular culture, is also closely connected to Torres García's lecture/manifesto 'The School of the South' (1944), in which the artist stated, 'I have called this "The School of the South" because, in reality, our north is the South. There must not be north for us, except in opposition to our South. Therefore, we now turn the map upside down, and then we have a true idea of our position, and not as the rest of the world wishes. The point of America, from now on, forever, insistently points to the South, our north'.

I decided to write a Shakespearean sonnet based on Torres García's famous artwork to explore this suggestive inversion, both visually but also semantically and conceptually, turning the gaze to some of the drawing's most arresting qualities, among them its rebelliousness and deceiving simplicity. My poem attempts to link the ideas behind this drawing with those of a rising Tiwanaku, the capital of a powerful pre-Hispanic empire that dominated a large area of the southern Andes and beyond, reaching its zenith between AD 500 and 900. It is a rendition of what I've called 'a bold experiment/of liberation, a flipped cosmology, a laboratory of the new'. The ekphrastic poem 'A Latin American Sonnet LXXXI' became part of a more extensive series of Sonnets I wrote for my second English collection that looks at all things Latin American and Latinx, from anthropological, scientific and historical standpoints, to the ecological, personal, cultural and political.

LORETTE C. LUZAJIC

Uncle Satan: Cerro Rico's Sympathy for the Devil

after El Tio effigy sculptures (Cerro Rico, Bolivia) past and contemporary

1. The devil is hung like a horse. Ramrod red, his prick protrudes between gangly splayed legs in rubber boots. He is festooned in rainbow ribbons. His effigy lurks in every mineshaft alcove under Cerro Rico. His sinister grin is stuffed with cigarettes. Lord of the Underworld, the devil squats on his throne of Puro empties.

2. *El Tio* loves beer and rubbing alcohol, but they're not his libation of choice. He is bloodthirsty. At the annual Carnaval, the Oruro and Potosi locals feast and dance with the devil. A big brass band makes merry as blindfolded llamas are wheeled in for slaughter. The yatiri, the witchdoctor, passes out knives. Miners brush their cheeks with llama blood. The rest is all for Uncle, so that he will be satiated and spare the workers their own.

3. It is not enough: El Tio wiggles filthy fingers. He wants more. The villagers rip *el corazon* from the beasts and kiss them, then offer them to Uncle. He likes his hearts still beating.

4. All night, there will be music and fires and drinking until obliteration. There will be saltenas, and tripe with peanut sauce, and llama charque and spicy llajua. There will be rostro asado, a whole sheep's head tenderized with a miner's blow torch.

5. The white ribbon clouds, the red dust roads. All is silent when the festival ends. Eternity spills from these barren hills, stretching ahead as dry and fruitless as the silver veins inside, below. Every miner dreams of that lucky strike. But after five centuries and 60,000 tons of silver excavation, only scraps remain.

6. Supay is an ancient god of the mines of the Andes in Inca and Quechua history. He was lord of the hills and lord of death long before the arrival of the Catholic devil. Supay is Uncle, or Uncle's helper, or manifest through Uncle, or Uncle's friend. Uncle is local to Cerro Rico, syncretized by Supay and Satan.

7. A little lead, a bit of zinc and tin. All that's left. Nearby Potosi, once the thriving Imperial City, is a remote and dusty ghost town. It was the jewel of New Spain and the colonial empire. Now that the mines are nearly bereft, El Tio's mountain finally belongs to the indigenous people of Bolivia. It is the burial ground for thousands of Brown and Black slaves. Many say the real devil is Spain.

8. A boy emerges from a crevice between rocks, pushing a wheelbarrow. Blistered hands, sandals tied by twine. Countless children work inside. The mountain that eats men, they say, men, and boys. Tattered rope ladders drop thirty feet into caverns too narrow for small men to crawl. Shafts crumble under dynamite and time. Miners crawl for miles on hands and knees. There are tunnels that lead where no one knows, where men disappear into the darkness.

9. The women from the villages wear long and layered prairie skirts and bowler hats. They bring booze, and coca leaves, water, empanadas, anticuchos. They pray to the Virgin of the Tunnels. They wait for their men and boys.

10. The worst way to die happens to all who survive the devil inside. *Silicosis.* Inhaling crystalline silica ravages the alveoli and slowly chokes a man to death. Those who evade collapses, explosions, rickets, starvation, injury, alcohol poisoning, and suffocation, will be dead from silicosis before they hit forty.

11. There are few statues or images of El Tio anywhere else. Only at Carnaval is the devil invited outside, when the annual dramas of good and evil involve him. Tourists take photos, but believers do not invite him outside on to God's land. The mines are the Uncle's realm. The villagers respect his kingdom. They pay the rent. They give the devil his due. They believe, because hell is real.

Commentary

It doesn't always take ten years to write a poem, but this one did.

In 2012, a stunning exhibition of colonial era silver from Peru came to my city of Toronto. I'm very interested in Latin American art and mythology, and silver is one of my passions, so this was an incredible experience. A silver mask of the terrifying Incan horned demon god of the mines, Supay, was the star of the show. I didn't have to dig far to find another fascinating figure related to Supay, still worshipped by remote mountain communities in Bolivia, nicknamed El Tio, or the Uncle.

I was moved by a film I found in my research, *The Devil's Miner* (2005), directed by Kief Davidson and Richard Ladkani, about the horrific conditions of the Cerro Rico silver mine workers. I learned about Spain's reign over the region and their rise in wealth and empire from Andean silver and the slave workers mining it. I began writing poetry inspired by the Supay mask and the movie. Words failed. How could I honor the victims of such unspeakable oppression?

The only thing I kept from the early scraps of this poem was the title 'Uncle Satan', because it had a bit of the dark wit and irreverence that I often relish. Nothing else stuck.

Some time later I was looking at medieval artwork of the Devil and hell. I saw Bosch paintings in person in Portugal and remarkable paintings in Spain. It struck me that the Dantean vision of hell looked a lot like the real world inside the Cerro Rico mines. The view of hell as a pit swallowing human bodies brought me back to that blank page.

The song by the Rolling Stones, 'Sympathy for the Devil', was a natural soundtrack. Not exactly a praise or worship hymn to the devil as the band was often accused, the song was inspired by the Soviet satire and literary masterpiece, *The Master and Margarita* by Mikhail Bulgakov. I struggle to better understand this complex work examining atheism, corruption, deception, censorship, and evil from many angles. But what I drew from the song is that we look to accuse 'the devil' anywhere and everywhere, forgetting that the mirror is the most certain place to find him.

This brought to my mind the strange rituals and effigies to El Tio petitioning his protection in the dangerous mines of Bolivia, religious art and myth born from terrible oppression. We may recoil at rites dismissed as superstitious, but yet here I am wearing armloads and handfuls of silver without flinching. The brutal enslavement of indigenous people and Africans in the silver mines by Spain gave me the line 'Many say the real devil is Spain'.

None of the fragments came together until the call for this project suggesting ekphrastic inspiration beyond visual art. This unwritten poem had been incubating for so long with so many diverse works of human creativity, including the labor of the miners bringing the beauty of silver to the world. I wondered whether the time for Uncle Satan had finally come. I found my way in when I saw some El Tio sculptures with a giant phallus. A bit of shock and humor allowed me to break the ice, so to speak.

I love to write prose poems that are also sectioned or lists. They reflect the disparate elements that come together to tell a story, like a scrapbook or collage of fragments suggesting a bigger picture.

This approach also reflected the different artistic influences drawn on for the poem, most of them behind the scenes. I immersed myself again in the harrowing elements, meditating on a photo of the silver Supay mask. I watched documentary footage. I watched the video 'La La La' by Naughty Boy, featuring Sam Smith, which includes a scene filmed with El Tio at Cerro Rico. I pondered as many film stills and photos of El Tio effigies as I could find. Finally, I found the words.

JEN WEBB

The One Who Falls

Because we are always on stage, or falling off the edge. Because when we reach the apogee all that's left is the nadir. You sit sulking on the plywood stairs while we busy ourselves around you, stumbling and then steadying, falling up; falling down.

That schmaltzy soundtrack, which once we scorned as poplit-light, which now we read as deep tragedy despite its bossa nova bounce. We would samba if we could, but instead must run, helping each another and hindering, learning anew what the laws of physics will do. Stumbling, tumbling, we run without pause, learn how to love and how to leave, find our way back to the balance point.

It's the March of history, says someone, it's the April May and June. Someone's phone is playing Bach's Toccata on tin piano and we all fall silent to listen. The music goes on. You stagger across to join us, and we take your hands, and we go on.

Catch your breath, dearest. No questions now, you say, knowing that our gift was of bodies that must die, and that dying leaves us nowhere else to go. Until then, you draw me in and we dance again, a choreography written by someone we don't know, by someone who knows what it takes to keep us on our feet.

Commentary

Shortly after I turned eight my ballet teacher had a serious conversation with my mother. I lacked, she said, the ballet ethos. I treated each class as an opportunity to make the other children laugh. I knocked over the sets at a public performance when my scarf-rainbow was caught in the construction, and all the dads in the audience laughed when they should have been applauding. My mother agreed; that was the end of my dance training.

It was the end, too, of any possible literacy with respect to dance. Yes, I've often attended performances of the Bolshoi Ballet or the Royal Ballet or the Australian Ballet, delighting in the colour and movement; I've been to experimental dance performances at arts festivals or in the small downstairs theatres at the Opera House. But I possess no criteria for judgment, and have no confidence that I could make any statement about a dance performance except: 'I like this one'; 'I didn't get that one'.

In 2016 I bumped into Yoann Bourgeois' *Celui qui tombe* (*He who falls*), a dance performance *cum* narrative that analogizes the pattern of human life: what he calls 'mankind in miniature'. The six dancers – three women, three men – emerge on a turntable that performs as their stage; turning, rocking, swaying. To the strains of Frank Sinatra's 'My Way', they walk – in ones and twos, or as a collective. They embrace, break away; run, and stumble, and find their feet again; jostle each other; delight in each other; separate into solitude; and then finally, one by one, they fall and stay fallen. As each goes down, the others keep running, stepping or jumping over their comrades. At last, only one dancer still perseveres, awkwardly, picking a path between the bodies of her companions, until finally she too falls. The stage keeps turning; the dancers are still.

I call them 'dancers', though really – in this and in other Bourgeois pieces – they are circus performers; performance artists; statements on the philosophy of embodiment. His corpus of work is marked by the presence of the body in the world, and the beautiful, awkward ways human bodies navigate space. In some pieces the characters hang onto swinging timber beams; or balance in giant WobblyMan suits, rolling toward and away from each other. In others they mount staircases that continually tip them off, or they enter and exit the stage through unexpected doors. They are always falling; sometimes arresting their fall, more often ragdolling down onto (presumably) a trampoline, and being ragdolled up again and back onto the set.

They fall, and land, like ragdolls possessed of the art of balance, whether in or out of balance. In his introduction to the anthology *Of the presence of the body* (2004),[1] André Lepecki writes in a manner that seems to describe Bourgeois' choreography:

> The phenomenological intertwining of presence and body that dance brings about as it moves ... brings about the current turn in dance studies toward the fields of performance studies and of critical theory. This turn is not at all smooth. It generated a space of dizziness – that space Gaston Bachelard once saw as the generative space of thought. (p. 2)

Yoann Bourgeois' approach to choreography and performance is characterized by the dizziness his dancers have noted; the dizziness he too identifies when he terms his work 'the games of vertigo'.[2] And this dizziness for me does what

1. Lepecki, André (ed.) 2004, *Of the presence of the body: Essays on dance and performance theory*, Middletown Connecticut: Wesleyan University Press.
2. Yoann Bourgeois, in Robb, Peter 2018 'NAC Dance: Yoann Bourgeois plays "vertigo games" as he looks for a true tipping point', *ARTSFILE* (8 March), https://artsfile.ca/nac-dance-yoann-bourgeois-plays-vertigo-games-as-he-looks-for-a-true-tipping-point/

Bachelard promised: it becomes a space of thought, and a space that generates other ways of thinking poetically, of writing poems. Perhaps because his is an art that is, as he insists, not about 'man' as 'the center of the universe ... the center of the stage'.[3] It is about the physics of (im)balance, and about the beauty of falling; and of falling as a way of flying.

Weight; gravity; balance; agility; fluidity; insouciance. This sort of being reminds me of how it might feel to be the one who falls; the one who lives marinading in optimism while living in failure; the one who believes we are all in flight before realizing that we are simply ragdolling through the world. The one who comes, perhaps gradually, to realize that the falling doesn't matter; that the joy of the moment, the brief instances of flight, are enough.

---

3. Szekeres, Joe 2018 'Review: "he who falls (celui qui tombe)" at Canadian Stage', *OnStage Blog*, 2 March, https://www.onstageblog.com/reviews/2018/3/2/review-he-who-falls-celui-qui-tombe-at-canadian-stage

Jo Clement

Existence

We are here, beside the Reichstag,
to present the signatures of the dead:

five hundred thousand, and more, float
down the Spree. We raked for names

and brought armfuls to this graveyard glade
they'd drive an S-Bahn through. A train

through a memorial, our daily grief.
With its coffee cups and stubs, Berlin Central

isn't far from here. Deutsche Bahn still clatters
human freight over Reichsbahn tracks.

Arrivals, fraught departures. Passing names.
Do not move, they say. Then in death, Go.

No. This place is our Karavan, sweet Sinti,
dear Roma. Here, a decade long,

the beaten heart persists. Over and over,
a violin slices a mournful minor note.

Let's whistle this pitch to the children,
and call them back. Each one remembered,

remembering. Faces pool in nightwater.
Every day, a fresh flower rises.

Commentary

Artworks in public spaces can take several years to come to fruition. Before they can begin making their interventions, artists often battle through funding competitions, permission requests and consultations. Between the conception and unveiling of Berlin's 'Memorial to the Sinti and Roma Victims of National Socialism', two decades passed. The creator of this commemorative space, UNESCO's first Artist for Peace, Dani Karavan (1930–2021) believes this time span was highly unusual for a project of this scope and size. Core obstacles included limited budget and intense bureaucracy. Planning progress stalled relentlessly due to protracted debates and delays. At one point, for instance, the position of a bus stop almost halted the installation entirely. Major conflicts arose, particularly around naming the memorial. The Ministry of Culture insisted it should include *Zigeuner*. A misnomer and racial slur, the word translates as 'Gypsy'. It was used in Nazi documentation to define, categorize and ultimately perform genocide upon the Sinti and Roma people. State advisors fought remonstrations by the Central Council of German Sinti and Roma. Figures became another issue. The Government were keen to suggest only 100,000 Sinti and Roma were executed. In liaison with the Holocaust Memorial Trust and the testimony of families and survivors, the Council advised this was a belittling underestimate. Half a million deaths would be closer to the grievous truth. Upon completion of the memorial in 2012, Israeli Jewish sculptor Karavan told Exberliner, 'in all of the discussions with the German administration, I took the side of the Sinti and Roma'.

A decade on, the Roma Trial organization commissioned me to write a poem to mark the second Roma Biennale in Berlin, and the multi-sensory memorial's tenth year. The space is leafy and contemplative. Santino Spinelli's compelling poem 'Auschwitz' is carved into stone slabs that encircle a deep pool of water. Here, groups and individuals gather to remember the dead. Some learn of the somber history for the first time. In the middle of the pool, a triangular plinth represents the black inverted badge used by the fascists to categorize and earmark so-called 'work-shy' and 'asocial' people. As I began writing about the significance of this place, a distressing besiegement emerged. Its permanence was seemingly up for debate. The site, it appeared, was now in the way of a new public transport project. Reichsbahn child company Deutsche Bahn AG wanted to relocate the memorial. During the Holocaust, the state rail company profited from transporting over eleven million human beings to concentration camps. Unmistakably gauche and deeply disrespectful, the company soon changed their tack. They only wanted to tunnel beneath the site. I could hear the Reichstag Fire rekindling. In the aftermath of that parliamentary fire, Hitler urged President Hindenburg to pass a decree that suspended civil liberties and gave the Government extensive powers to suppress political opposition. The Nazis first abolished free speech, public assembly and fair trials. Death camps followed. With this context, my poem preserves the experience of watching a flower rise on the triangular plinth as a gesture of renewed remembrance. It became an ekphrasis less concerned with bringing visual art into figurative language or attempting to make Karavan's artwork speak. Instead, I speak up for it, in solidarity with the millions of marginalized and displaced Roma and Sinti. 'Existence' sends a message to states worldwide: the history and presence of Gypsy, Roma, and Traveller peoples cannot be erased.

DENISE DUHAMEL

The Nude

Emma Thompson says on *The Late Show with Stephen Colbert*,
"Don't waste your life's purpose worrying about your body."
She's there to promote a movie, *Good Luck To You, Leo Grande*,
in which she takes off all her clothes and stands in front
of a full-length mirror. She explains that she posed like Eve
in medieval paintings, relaxed with one knee slightly bent.
No shame, a neutral gaze. Her body was a body, like mine,
as Emma Thompson and I are both in our sixties.
It was a gift to the audience, she explains. Radical really.
In grad school, I took an art class in which one of the assignments
was self-portraiture. I too stood nude in front of a mirror
then sketched my breasts, my belly. I didn't know yet
how to draw faces so I cut off my head and legs, kept them
out of the frame. I drew the big round places of my body
and painted them aqua, which I thought was artsy. I remember
the professor's critique—"Try to be more vulnerable"—
which made me defensive. I'd just painted my boobs! She went on
to comment on the flatness, the color. I was blue like a cartoon
rather than fleshy. This was years before my abdomen scar
but I still wasted so much time hating my stomach. I loved food
too much to be an anorexic. A bulimic girl I knew
had died that year of a heart attack—How about that
as wasting her life's purpose? At the funeral
I didn't know what to say to her parents. Her chubby mother
seemed to blame herself. I was chubby too and felt extremely
vulnerable that day, then vulnerable again when the professor

told me I needed to be more vulnerable. The more my body
ages, the less I hate it even though (according to society's
standards) it loses more cachet every year I live in it.
Emma Thompson plays Nancy Stokes, a widow
who, though married for 31 years, never had an orgasm.
Leo Grande (Daryl McCormack) is a young sex worker
Nancy can barely afford. He is kind, exceedingly good
at his job. Marilyn Monroe once admitted to her psychiatrist
she'd never orgasmed either. So sex symbol or retired teacher,
it doesn't much matter. Some women hover, orgasm-less,
above their own bodies. Isabel Allende was asked at a Q&A
her biggest regret. She said that as a young woman
she should have had more sex. The college students
erupted with laughter and clapping. And I thought of that
time I wanted to go home with a guy but I was feeling fat
so declined. I admit I was jealous of the young woman
in that art class with her skinny arms and black straight bangs,
the young woman who received the most praise
for her self-portrait. Our professor gushed, "Ah, the metaphor,
the commentary on female beauty standards, consumerism,
with a throwback to Cinderella." I can still see
the oversized charcoal drawing of the student's favorite shoe,
a Guess open-toe sandal decorated with a rosette.

Commentary

My friend Angie told me she'd seen Emma Thompson's interview with Stephen Colbert and burst into tears. I looked it up on YouTube and had a similar reaction. How much more could I (and every woman I ever knew) have done with our lives if we didn't waste so much time worrying about our hair, waistlines, teeth, ankles, etc.? And later in life, our wrinkles and grays? Of course, I watched *Good Luck To You, Leo Grande* the very next night on Hulu. I paused on the scene Thompson talked about in her interview, amazed at the "gift" she gives to the audience, staring at herself, nude, in a full-length mirror at an age at which many women start to feel invisible. And yes—she IS posing like a medieval Eve! All people are deserving of love, sex, and pleasure, of course. But often art (especially visual art and film) fetishizes the young, the perfect, those the male gaze find most desirable. It's not surprising that *Good Luck To You, Leo Grande* was conceived by women—written by England's Katy Brand and directed by Australia's Sophie Hyde.

It's old news now that the camera is male, but I can't help but think of Laura Mulvey's 1975 essay, "Visual Pleasure and Narrative Cinema", in which she argues "the male figure cannot bear the burden of sexual objectification." So, if women are more likely the ones to be "seen" unclothed in film, how does feminism accommodate that reality? It seems to me that *Good Luck To You, Leo Grande* is one way. Spoiler alert—when Emma Thompson's character achieves her first orgasm she is looking at Daryl McCormack's character who is across the room. The script is flipped, so to speak.

I used *Good Luck To You, Leo Grande* as a point of departure to write about my own attempts at making narrative visual art—short lived, in grad school—and the problems of self-representation in a visual medium. This ekphrasis poem was also a way to explore the insecurities I feel about my own body, then and now. Emma Thompson's character actually says she has "always been ashamed of [her] body." That statement made me look back at that haunting memory of my grad school art class. The professor never said anything negative about my body, but I took in her comments as a stinging rebuke of my actual breasts and stomach. Not all of us will get a version of the too-good-to-be-true sex worker Leo Grande to help us overcome our woes, but I found the charm of this film to be its frank look at the baggage we all bring to body image and, by extension, sex.

John McCullough

Interview with the West Pier

Thank you for agreeing to this interview for the archive.
We are a museum of shadows. It seemed polite.

Would you say you identify as a crowd?
If the crowd is drowning: yes. Also: if the crowd is on fire.

Did queer visitors dance on you, clasp hands in the dark?
Pull the sadness out like magicians' scarves.

This is a story of despair?
The moon is an ambulance that will not find us.

Letters mention epiphanies – have you felt like a church?
Our starlings are angels, shitting everywhere.

The shadows recall no revelations?
You have not listened to a word we say.

And what of the future?
We are utterly ruined, and so we can begin.

Commentary

'Interview with the West Pier' is part of a sequence I've been working on over the last couple of years which engages with local history. It responds to the architecture of the West Pier, a construction situated on Brighton beach which opened in 1866 but which has been closed to the public since 1975. During the last few decades, the pier has gradually collapsed into the sea and it exists now only as a partial metal framework.

The first poem in the sequence, 'The West Pier Pays a Visit', imagined the pier visiting me in Watford before I moved to Brighton as a young man. There, it represented the city as a haven for queer exiles, those who leave their homes in search of somewhere to live their lives more freely. Here, the pier's representation of Brighton as a place where alternative sexualities can blossom is complicated by the presence of an archivist asking it questions about the past where, even in this city, there were severe restrictions on how much of themselves queer couples could display in public.

Many years ago, I worked as a volunteer at Brighton OurStory, an LGBT archive which gathered letters, magazines, flyers and other documents linked to Brighton as a center where queerness could be expressed. I was struck by how stubbornly evasive the letters could be, even after avowals of love, and of course these were the work of the brave few who left any trace at all. When funding was cut, the archive's collection was broken up and now it, too, exists solely in the memory of myself and a handful of others. There is an overwhelming sense of shadowiness about queer history, glimpses of a vast multitude of people whose lives were highly constrained and who could act on so few of their desires. The pier's darkness, its isolation, and the fact it is covered in starling droppings for me give it potential as a metaphor to express a little of all this.

I deliberately structured the poem as a dialogue because I wanted to capture also something of the elusive nature of queer history. The pier's answers to the archivist's questions are often cryptic whilst at the same time remaining suggestive of strong emotion. The last line carries a sense that, even though the pier is seemingly beyond rescue and queer histories often seem lost, the widening interest in the stories contained in both means that they still have useful roles to play as metaphors and reinforcers of identity for future generations.

Jacqueline Saphra

Le Rêve

after Picasso

Whose *rêve* is this? Or is it a joke, a code in fact,
your clean-cleaved scalpel-accurate *visage* split,
only the red urge of your *bouche* intact? Captured
in a languish, somewhat *deshabillée*, swooned
on *fauteuil rouge*, your fingers pointing pointedly
to shape a – yes, a *chatte* – lilac shoulders rounded
to the slip of straps, you must be somewhat cramped
Marie-Thérèse, neck folded sideways, a single sphere
of breast exposed, your nipple's one eye peeking
out at Pablo's back, his palette crazed with risk.

A man in a mac hovers far too near me, breathing
on the canvas; everybody wants to be your guest.
The crowd thrusts forward but I stand my ground
to puzzle at your sectioned face, I stare and blur
till truth patches into focus and suddenly it's obvious.

Marie-Thérèse, wake up

it's Twenty-Nineteen, the breathing men are breathing
on your skin in perpetuity and yes, believe it, half your face,
your lovely face, Marie-Thérèse, is here *depicted as a penis*.
Once seen, you cannot possibly unsee it.

Jesus, Marie-Thérèse, look at the canvas, you abject,
object visual pun, soft mistress of the cock-eyed beast

do not dream on,
      wake up, wake up, Marie-Thérèse and run.

Commentary

In spring 2018 I went to the Tate Gallery to see an exhibition called 'Love, Fame, Tragedy', billed as 'A month-by-month journey through Picasso's "Year of Wonders", 1932'. I had always had an ambivalent relationship with Picasso. My late stepfather was a Picasso-obsessed artist. Childhood camping trips through Europe were always punctuated by his pilgrimages to see the great works, which to me translated into endless boring afternoons in art galleries.

The main theme of the works in the Tate was Picasso's secret affair with the twenty-two year old Marie-Thérèse Walter who is considered to be the model – or at least the inspiration – for many of them. Picasso was still married to Olga Khokhlova who had been his principal muse until Marie-Thérèse arrived. One of the paintings, *Woman with Dagger*, shows a woman murdering her sexual rival; no need for any interpretation of this very literal fantasy.

This was indeed a year of Love, Fame and Tragedy, but the 'tragedy' was evidently not Picasso's. The world was descending into fascism, the women he was involved with were struggling, but Picasso was, as they put it in the Tate guide, 'an international superstar'. All this against the background of the Spanish Civil War (which he portrayed in his masterwork 'Guernica') and the depression engulfing the US and Europe. At the time of painting *Le Rêve*, Picasso was at the height of his fame and ostentatiously enjoying the money and prestige—his Savile Row suits, his chauffeured car and his lavish lifestyle. His paintings were fetching record prices but he was insecure about his position all the same.

My fascination with ekphrastic art invariably lies in the ways that art and life intersect. I had already experienced a strong reaction to the exhibition, the tone of the commentary and the paintings that had been created too quickly by an artist who felt he was beyond criticism. By the time I looped back to *Le Rêve*, the painting chosen for the exhibition poster, I was in a mild state of rage. I approached it as I invariably approach a painting I want to write towards: with a watchful, enquiring mind, but also open to the emotional impact. I examined it in detail, I entered it as a person might enter a room. I began to feel enraged that Picasso considered Marie-Thérèse to be his object, that in some way he owned her and could mold her into whatever he wanted on the canvas. It's worth saying that I was coming from the place of someone who, as a child, has observed her own mother being betrayed repeatedly by a womanizing artist. This is a familiar trope: the genius who is so free and wild, so gifted, his behavior is always considered justified and excused because of his genius.

My tour around the painting begins by describing what I see in it: and I deliberately allow my subjective experience of it to enter the discourse. In the second stanza I place myself as the viewer in the art gallery, I describe part of the awkwardness of being a woman in a confined public space alongside male strangers viewing a series of highly erotic nudes. It's then that the painting begins to come into focus, and the poem charts my slow realization of what I am looking at. This is a nude painting of a woman whose head is *partly a penis!* Picasso is claiming his erotic ownership of Marie-Thérèse by replacing part of her with a ridiculous representation of his masculinity. I want her to get out of the chair, get out of the room, get out of the painting. And she's not the only woman who should wake up and run: as evidenced by recent events in Hollywood and in politics, the power dynamic hasn't shifted much in the past hundred years.

The poem took several years to arrive at itself with a few key elements finally coming together: my own subjective experience, the historical background, the context of the exhibition as a whole, and of course the painting itself. A poem that began as an exploration of an artwork from 1932 fed right into my present, my politics, and became a feminist critique of 'the male artist', the art world and the behaviors it still tolerates.

Biographical Notes

Amina Alyal publishes poetry widely, e.g. in *Iota, Dream Catcher, Metamorphic: 21st Century Poets Respond to Ovid*, and two collections, *The Ordinariness of Parrots* (Stairwell Books, 2015) and *Season of Myths* (Wordspace/Indigo Dreams, 2016). She has published scholarly research, e.g. editing *Speaking Picture and Silent Text* with Cambridge Scholars (2023). She often works with ekphrastic and synaesthetic cross-overs.

Sally Ashton is a writer, teacher, and editor in chief of DMQ Review, an online journal featuring poetry and art. Author of four books, Ashton specializes in brief forms across genres and in collaboration with artists. A fifth collection, *Listening to Mars*, is forthcoming, 2024. One of her poems was selected to go to the Moon as part of the Lunar Codex.

Cassandra Atherton is an award-winning prose poet and international expert on prose poetry. She co-authored *Prose Poetry: An Introduction* (Princeton UP) and co-edited the *Anthology of Australian Prose Poetry* (Melbourne UP) and is currently writing a book of prose poetry on the atomic bomb with funding from the Australia Council. Cassandra is a commissioning editor for *Westerly* magazine, senior editor at *Spinless Wonders* and has her own imprint at MadHat Press (USA).

Mary Jo Bang is the author of nine books of poems—including *A Film in Which I Play Everyone, A Doll for Throwing*, and *Elegy*, which received the National Book Critics Circle Award. She has published translations of Dante's *Inferno*, illustrated by Henrik Drescher, *Purgatorio*, and *Colonies of Paradise: Poems by Matthias Göritz*. She teaches at Washington University in St. Louis. Her translation of *Paradiso* is forthcoming from Graywolf Press in 2025.

Stuart Barnes is the author of *Like to the Lark* (Upswell Publishing, 2023) winner of the 2023 Wesley Michel Wright Prize in Poetry, and *Glasshouses* (UQP, 2016), winner of the 2015 Arts Queensland Thomas Shapcott Poetry Prize, commended for the 2016 Anne Elder Award and shortlisted for the 2017 Mary Gilmore Award. Stuart, Nigel Featherstone, Melinda Smith and CJ Bowerbird are Hell Herons, a spoken-work/music collective whose first record is due in 2024. www.stuartabarnes.com

Janée J. Baugher, MFA, is the author of the only craft book of its kind, *The Ekphrastic Writer: Creating Art-Influenced Poetry, Fiction and Nonfiction*, as well as the ekphrastic poetry collections *The Body's Physics* and *Coördinates of Yes*. She's an assistant editor at Boulevard magazine, and she's been featured on Seattle Channel TV and at the Library of Congress. www.JaneeBaugher.com

Bob Beagrie, PhD, lives in Middlesbrough. He is a poet, playwright and performer. Previous publications include: *The Last Almanac* (Yaffle Press, 2023), *When We Wake We Think We're Whalers from Eden* (Stairwell Books, 2021), *And Then We Saw The Daughter of the Minotaur* (The Black Light Engine Press, 2020), *Civil Insolencies* (Smokestack, 2019).

Bina is a poet, founder-editor-designer and publisher of the award-winning *International Gallerie*, a global arts and ideas journal encouraging unity in diversity. She is also an art curator and fiction writer. She has had seven books of poems published. Many of her poems have been translated into Mandarin, Spanish, French, Greek, Arabic and Urdu. Bina is a nomad who lives and works from Mumbai, India.

Linda Black is Editor of *Long Poem Magazine*: http://longpoemmagazine.org.uk A poet and artist, she has published five collections, the latest being *Then* (Shearsman Books, 2021) – a collection of ekphrastic poems is forthcoming. Her etchings/drawings appear on all book covers. *The Son of a Shoemaker* (Hearing Eye, 2012), illustrated prose-poems about the early life of Hans Andersen, was the subject of a Poetry Society exhibition.

246

Leo Boix is a bilingual Latinx poet born in Argentina who lives in the UK. His debut English collection *Ballad of a Happy Immigrant* (Vintage, 2021) was awarded the Poetry Book Society Wild Card Choice. He was the recipient of the Bart Wolffe Poetry Prize Award, the Keats-Shelley Prize, a PEN Award, and the Society of Authors' Foundation and K. Blundell Trust.

Jane Burn is an award-winning working-class, pansexual, autistic poet, artist and essayist. Her poems are widely published. Jane has an MA in Writing Poetry from Newcastle University and was awarded the 2022 academic prize for best overall performance. In 2023 she was awarded a grant by the RLF. Her latest collection, *Be Feared*, is available from Nine Arches.

Anne Caldwell is a writer and editor based in West Yorkshire, England. She is also an advisory fellow for the Royal Literary Fund. She is passionate about prose poetry and writing about place. Her latest book is *Alice and the North* (Valley Press, 2020). She has also co-edited a book of essays with Oz Hardwick, *Prose Poetry Theory and Practice* (Routledge, 2022). Anne's work has been widely published in Australia, the UK, and the United States. www.annecaldwell.net

Jo Clement lives in Newcastle, England. They are a Northern Writers' Award winner and teach Creative Writing at Northumbria University. BBC Radio appearances include *Enchanted Isle, Northern Drift, Poetry Please,* and **Start the Week**. Their debut collection *Outlandish* (Bloodaxe Books, 2022) is shortlisted for the John Pollard International Poetry Prize. www.joclement.co.uk.

Simon Collings lives in Oxford, UK. His poetry, short fiction, translations, reviews and essays have appeared in a wide range of magazines. A collection of his prose poems and short fiction, *Why are you here?*, was published by Odd Volumes in November 2020. His third chapbook, *Sanchez Ventura*, was published by Leafe Press in spring 2021. He is a contributing editor at *The Fortnightly Review*. More information at: https://simoncollings.wordpress.com/

Denise Duhamel's most recent books of poetry are *Second Story* (Pittsburgh, 2021) and *Scald* (2017). *Blowout* (2013) was a finalist for the National Book Critics Circle Award. A recipient of fellowships from the Guggenheim Foundation and the National Endowment for the Arts, she is a distinguished university professor in the MFA program at Florida International University in Miami.

Ian Duhig became a full-time writer after working with homeless people for fifteen years. A Fellow of the Royal Society of Literature and former International Writer Fellow at Trinity College Dublin, Duhig has won the Forward Best Poem Prize once, the National Poetry Competition twice and his *New and Selected Poems* from Picador received the 2022 Hawthornden Prize for Literature.

Moira Egan's most recent volume is *Amore e Morte* (*Love and Death*), a bilingual poetry collection (Edizioni Tlon, Rome). Her work has been published in journals and anthologies on four continents. She has been a Mid Atlantic Arts Foundation Fellow at the Virginia Center for the Creative Arts and has held writing fellowships at the St. James Cavalier Centre for Creativity, Malta; the Civitella Ranieri Center; the Rockefeller Foundation Bellagio Center; and the James Merrill House. She lives, teaches, and sometimes even writes in Rome.

Niloofar Fanaiyan is a writer and poet currently residing in Haifa, Israel. She was the 2016 Donald Horne Research Fellow at the Centre for Creative and Cultural Research, University of Canberra, where she obtained her PhD. She received the Canberra Critics Circle Literary Award for Poetry for her book of poems titled *Transit* (RWP, 2016).

Toby Fitch is poetry editor of *Overland* and a lecturer in creative writing at the University of Sydney. He is the author of eight books of poetry, including *Where Only the Sky Had Hung Before* (Vagabond Press, 2019), *Sydney Spleen* (Giramondo Publishing, 2021), and, most recently, a newly expanded and full-color edition of *Object Permanence: Calligrammes* (Puncher & Wattmann/Thorny Devil

Press, December 2022). He co-edited *Best of Australian Poetry 2021* with Ellen van Neerven, and edited the anthology *Groundswell: The Overland Judith Wright Poetry Prize for New & Emerging Poets 2007–2020*. He lives in Sydney on unceded Gadigal land.

Hedy Habra is the author of four poetry collections, most recently, *Or Did You Ever See The Other Side?*; *The Taste of the Earth*, a Silver Nautilus Book Award Winner and Eric Hoffer Award Honorable Mention; *Tea in Heliopolis* won the Best Book Award; and *Under Brushstrokes* was a Finalist for the International Book Award. She is a twenty-one-time nominee for the Pushcart Prize and Best of the Net. https://www.hedyhabra.com/

Oz Hardwick is a European poet and academic, whose work has been widely published in international journals and anthologies. He has published twelve full collections and chapbooks, most recently *A Census of Preconceptions* (SurVision, 2022), which was shortlisted for the 2023 Rubery International Book Award for poetry. He also has written extensively on Creative Writing, poetry, the Middle Ages, medievalism, and other obsessive interests. Oz is Professor of Creative Writing at Leeds Trinity University. www.ozhardwick.co.uk

Jennifer Harrison has written eight books of poetry, most recently *Anywhy* (Black Pepper 2018). She manages The Dax Poetry Collection housed in the Dax Centre at the University of Melbourne and in 2012 received the Christopher Brennan Award for sustained achievement in Australian poetry. Her ninth collection *Sideshow History* is forthcoming in 2023.

Dominique Hecq writes across genres and disciplines. Her most recent publications, including *Songlines* (Hedgehog, 2023) and *Endgame with No Ending* (SurVision, 2023), explore and explode the limits of the prose poem. Among other honors, Dominique Hecq is a recipient of the International Best Poets Prize administered by the International Poetry Translation and Research Centre in conjunction with the International Academy of Arts and Letters.

Bob Heman's words have been translated into Spanish, Arabic, Farsi, Italian, and Hungarian. His art includes collages, ink drawings, and participatory "cut-out" multiples on paper. He lives on the west end of Long Island in what was once the city of Brooklyn.

DeWitt Henry's books include *Restless for Words: Poems* (Finishing Line Press, 2023) and *Foundlings: Found Poems from Prose* (Gazebo, 2022). *Trim Reckonings: Poems* is forthcoming from Pierian Springs Press. He was the founding editor of *Ploughshares* and is Prof. Emeritus at Emerson College. Details at www.dewitthenry.com.

Paul Hetherington has published 18 full-length collections of poetry, including *Sleeplessness* (Pierian Springs Press, 2023). His poetry has won or been nominated for over 40 national and international awards and competitions. He is co-founding editor of the international online journal *Axon: Creative Explorations.* With Professor Cassandra Atherton he co-authored the authoritative 344-page *Prose Poetry: An Introduction* (Princeton UP, 2020) and co-edited the definitive *Anthology of Australian Prose Poetry* (Melbourne UP, 2020).

Kane Holborn writes poetry through the lens of visual art. Holborn's work is deeply rooted in ekphrastic practices about how disability images like his own are often misrepresented and airbrushed out of the proverbial picture. As a lover of art across all spectrums he is fascinated by color in both poetic and artistic contexts.

Sarah Holland-Batt is the author of three books of poems—most recently, *The Jaguar*—and a book of essays, *Fishing for Lightning.* Among other honours, she has been awarded the Prime Minister's Literary Award for Poetry and the Stella Prize. She is presently Professor of Creative Writing at QUT.

Holly Iglesias' work includes three poetry collections—*Souvenirs of Shrunken World, Angles of Approach,* and *Sleeping Things*—and a critical work, *Boxing Inside the Box: Women's Prose Poetry.* Her current projects are *Theories of Flight,* an intergenerational memoir, and *Dear Everybody 1947*, an annotated collection of letters between her mother and several friends who were co-workers during WWII.

Helen Ivory is a poet and collage artist who also makes shadow-boxes. Her fifth Bloodaxe collection is *The Anatomical Venus* (2019). She edits the webzine *Ink Sweat and Tears* and teaches creative writing online for the UEA/NCW. A book of mixed media poems, *Hear What the Moon Told Me*, is published by KFS, and chapbook *Maps of the Abandoned City* by SurVision. She also has work translated into Polish, Ukrainian, Spanish, Greek and Croatian as part of *Versopolis*. *Wunderkammer: New and Selected Poems* (2023) is published in the U.S. by MadHat Press. She was awarded Arts Council of England to research and write her next collection for Bloodaxe, *Constructing a Witch* (2024) which fixes on the monstering and scapegoating of women.

Andy Jackson is a poet, creative writing teacher and mentor, and a Patron of Writers Victoria. He was the inaugural Writing the Future of Health Fellow, and has co-edited disability-themed issues of *Southerly* and *Australian Poetry Journal*. Andy's latest poetry collection is *Human Looking*, which won the ALS Gold Medal and the Prime Minister's Literary Award for Poetry.

Luke Kennard is a poet and novelist who lives in Birmingham. His most recent collection, *Notes on the Sonnets* (Penned in the Margins, 2021), won the Forward Prize in 2021.

Nathan Langston is a Product Designer in Seattle. He is Director of Psychopomp Projects, a boutique production focused on cross-disciplinary works and was Director of TELEPHONE, an ekphrastic game played by almost 1000 artists in 476 cities in 72 countries.

Michael Leong is Robert P. Hubbard Assistant Professor of Poetry at Kenyon College. He has previously taught at SUNY Albany and California Institute of the Arts. His most recent books include *Words on Edge* (Black Square Editions, 2018) and *Contested Records:*

The Turn to Documents in Contemporary North American Poetry (University of Iowa Press, 2020).

Rupert M. Loydell is a Senior Lecturer at Falmouth University, the editor of *Stride* magazine, and contributing editor to *International Times*. He is a widely published poet whose most recent poetry book is *The Age of Destruction and Lies* (Shearsman, 2023). He has edited anthologies for Salt, Shearsman and KFS, written for academic journals such as *Punk & Post-Punk* (which he is on the editorial board of), and contributed to books about David Lynch, Brian Eno and Industrial music.

Lorette C. Luzajic is the founding editor of *The Ekphrastic Review*, the flagship journal of ekphrasis. She writes, publishes, edits, and teaches ekphrastic writing, art appreciation, flash fiction, prose poetry, and mixed media art. She is an international award-winning artist, with collectors in 30 countries so far.

Lisa Matthews is a poet, textual and asemic artist and digital content designer. Her doctoral research looks at how the *present text* (a new writing method explored in her PhD) can help transform life experience into writing practice. You can see her work on Instagram @copperhart_arts and @voila_ici. Her latest book, *Darlings, Deletions*, is available from: nightowlbookshop.com

John McCullough's book of poems, *Reckless Paper Birds*, was published with Penned in the Margins. It won the 2020 Hawthornden Prize for Literature as well as being shortlisted for the Costa Poetry Award. His poem 'Flower of Sulphur' was shortlisted for the 2021 Forward Prize for Best Single Poem. His latest collection, *Panic Response*, was a Book of the Year in *The Telegraph* as well as being included in *The Times'* list of Notable New Poetry Books of 2022. He lives in Hove and teaches at the University of Brighton and for the Arvon Foundation.

Jane Monson is a Specialist Mentor for disabled students at the University of Cambridge and independent scholar. She edited British

Prose Poetry: The Poems without Lines (Palgrave 2018). Her solo collections include *Speaking Without Tongues, The Shared Surface* and *The Chalk Butterfly*. She is currently working on a fourth.

Paul Munden is a poet, editor and screenwriter living in North Yorkshire. He has published six poetry collections, including *Amplitude* (Recent Work Press, 2022), and has just completed a book on violinist Nigel Kennedy. He was director of the UK's National Association of Writers in Education, 1994–2018, and is now an Adjunct Associate Professor at the University of Canberra, Australia.

Alvin Pang, PhD, is a Singaporean poet and editor whose writings have been translated into more than twenty languages worldwide, including Swedish, Macedonian and Chinese. A 2022 Dublin Literary Award judge, Civitella Ranieri Fellow and Adjunct Professor of RMIT University, his recent books include *Uninterrupted time* (2019), *Det som ger oss våra namn* (2022), and *Diaphanous* (2023; with George Szirtes).

In 1998, **Jonathan Penton** founded UnlikelyStories.org, an electronic journal of literature and art, and its daughter imprint, Unlikely Books, in 2005. Since then, he has lent editorial, management, and technical assistance to a number of literary and artistic ventures, such as the New Orleans Poetry Festival, MadHat, Inc., and *Rigorous*. He has organized literary performances, and performed himself, around North America.

Pascale Petit's eighth collection, *Tiger Girl* (Bloodaxe, 2020), was shortlisted for the Forward Prize and for Wales Book of the Year. Her seventh, *Mama Amazonica* (Bloodaxe, 2017), won the inaugural Laurel Prize and the Ondaatje Prize. Four collections were shortlisted for the T.S. Eliot Prize, including *What the Water Gave Me: Poems after Frida Kahlo* (Seren, 2010). Trained as a sculptor at the Royal College of Art, she spent the first part of her life as a visual artist.

Felicity Plunkett is a poet and critic. Her books are *A Kinder Sea* (UQP), *Vanishing Point* (UQP) and the chapbook *Seastrands*

(Vagabond). Felicity was UQP's Poetry Editor for a decade and edited *Thirty Australian Poets* (UQP). She has a PhD from the University of Sydney and is a widely published reviewer and essayist.

Kristin Sanders is an American writer based in Paris. Her books include *CUNTRY*, a finalist for the 2015 National Poetry Series, and two poetry chapbooks: *Orthorexia*, and *This is a map of their watching me*. Her work has recently been published in *Prose Poetry: An Introduction* (Princeton UP, 2020) and the international anthology *Alcatraz* (Gazebo Books, 2022).

Jacqueline Saphra is a poet, playwright, teacher and activist. She is the author of five chapbooks and four poetry collections. Her second collection *All My Mad Mothers* was shortlisted for the T.S. Eliot Prize and her fifth, *Velvel's Violin*, a Poetry Book Society Recommendation, was published in 2023. Jacqueline is a founder member of Poets for the Planet.

Ian Seed's recent publications include *The Underground Cabaret* (prose poems) (Shearsman, 2020), *Operations of Water* (verse poems) (KF&S, 2020), *The Dice Cup* (prose poems from the French of Max Jacob) (Wakefield Press, US, 2022) and *The River Which Sleep Has Told Me* (verse poems from the Italian of Ivano Fermini) (*Fortnightly Review* Odd Volumes, 2022). *Night Window* is out from Shearsman in early 2024.

Sudeep Sen is one of the leading international poets whose prize-winning books include: *Postmarked India: New & Selected Poems* (HarperCollins), *Rain, Aria* (A. K. Ramanujan Translation Award), *Fractals: New & Selected Poems | Translations 1980–2015* (London Magazine Editions), *EroText* (Vintage: Penguin Random House), *Kaifi Azmi: Poems | Nazms* (Bloomsbury) and *Anthropocene: Climate Change, Contagion, Consolation* (Pippa Rann, 2021–22 Rabindranath Tagore Literary Prize winner). Sen's works have been translated into over 25 languages.

Ruth Stacey is a poet from Worcester, England. She is the author of *Queen, Jewel, Mistress* (2015), *I, Ursula* (2020), *Viola the Virgin Queen* (2021), and *The Dark Room: Letters to Krista* (2021). Stacey is currently writing the imagined memoirs of the tarot artist Pamela Colman Smith.

Edwin Stockdale was the first person to gain a PhD in Creative Writing (Poetry) from Leeds Trinity University. Red Squirrel Press have published two pamphlets, *Aventurine* (2014) and *The Glower of the Sun* (2019), with a third due out next year. Currently, he is completing his debut collection about the bisexual medieval monarch Edward II, funded by Arts Council England.

Cole Swensen is the author of 20 books of poetry, most recently *Art In Time* (Nightboat Books, 2021). A former Guggenheim Fellow, recipient of the Iowa Poetry Prize, the SF State Poetry Center Book Award, the National Poetry Series, and the PEN USA Award in translation, she teaches at Brown University and divides her time between France and the US.

Marc Vincenz is an Anglo-Swiss-American poet, fiction writer, translator, editor, publisher, musician and artist. He has published over thirty books of poetry, fiction and translation including more recently, *A Brief Conversation with Consciousness*, *There Might be a Moon or a Dog*, *The Little Book of Earthly Delights* and *The Pearl Diver of Irunmani*. His work has been translated into many languages, including German, Romanian, Italian, Chinese and Japanese. Vincenz is editor and publisher of MadHat Press, publisher of *New American Writing*.

Jen Webb is Distinguished Professor of Creative Practice at University of Canberra. Author or editor of 30 scholarly volumes, she has also published 18 poetry collections and artist books, and is co-editor of the Mandarin/English anthology *Open Windows: Contemporary Australian Poetry*. Her recent poetry collections are *Moving Targets* (Recent Work Press, 2018); and, with Shé Hawke, *Flight Mode* (RWP, 2020).

Originally from the UK, **Mags Webster** now lives in Western Australia. Her first poetry book *The Weather of Tongues* won Australia's national Anne Elder Award for best debut collection in 2011. Her next collection, *Nothing to Declare*, was shortlisted in the 2021 Prime Minister's Literary Awards.

Jessica L. Wilkinson is the author of three poetic biographies, most recently *Music Made Visible: A Biography of George Balanchine* (Vagabond, 2019). She is the founding editor of *Rabbit: a journal for nonfiction poetry* and an associate professor in Writing and Publishing at RMIT University, Melbourne.

Jane Yeh's collection *Discipline* (Carcanet, 2019) was a Poetry Book Society Recommendation. She was named a Next Generation poet by the PBS for *The Ninjas* (2012), while her first collection, *Marabou* (2005), was shortlisted for the Forward, Whitbread, and Aldeburgh poetry prizes.

Printed in the USA
CPSIA information can be obtained
at www.ICGtesting.com
CBHW032343070424
6549CB00003B/19